Why Daily Handwriting Practice?

The premise behind *Daily Handwriting Practice* is simple and straightforward—frequent, focused practice of a skill leads to mastery and retention of that skill.

What's in *Daily Handwriting Practice?*

The book is divided into 36 weekly sections. Practice for Monday through Thursday includes half pages on which students practice writing letters, words, and sentences. Friday's practice involves a full page.

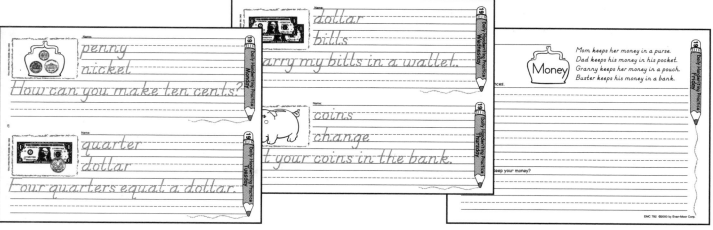

Daily Handwriting Practice is more than handwriting.

Students are practicing a variety of important vocabulary words:

color words	months
number words—cardinal and ordinal	sports
verbs	position words
animal names	family members
days of the week	

As they write and read words in context, students are learning about curriculum topics:

nutrition	the continents
the solar system	geometric shapes
the layers of the earth	money
recycling	energy
fractions	

1

Daily Handwriting Practice

D1397090

Letter Formation Chart

Aa Bb Cc Dd

Ee Ff Gg Hh

Ii Jj Kk Ll

Mm Nn Oo Pp

Qq Rr Ss Tt

Uu Vv Ww Xx

Yy Zz

Daily Handwriting Practice • EMC 792

anteater

A A A

a a a

Aa Aa

AA aa

3

Name:

bat

B B B

b b b

Bb Bb

AB ab

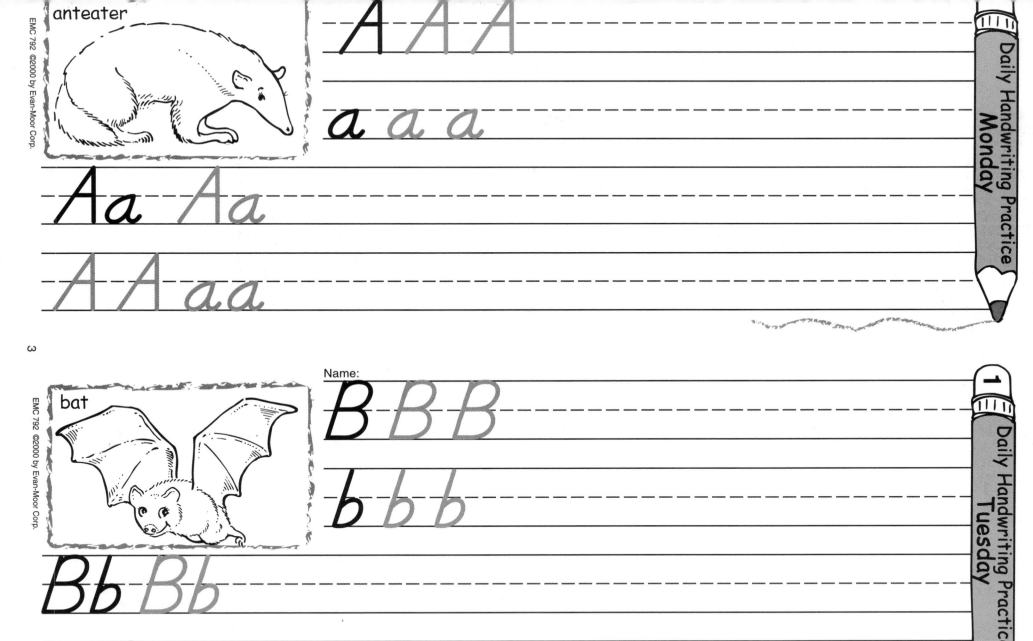

ABCD abcd

Dd Dd Dd

P P P
P P P

D D D
D D D

Name:

dog

4

ABC abc

Cc Cc

c c c

C C C

Name:

cat

Aa   Bb   Cc   Dd

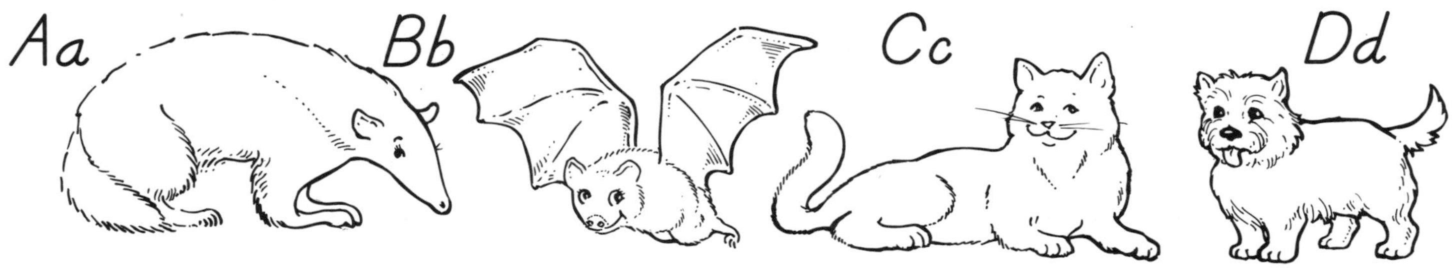

Copy the letters.

Aa

Bb

Cc

Dd

Dad   *bad*

dab   *cab*

elephant

Name:

E E E

e e e

Ee Ee

a b c d e

6

fox

Name:

F F F

f f f

Ff Ed Dd

Cc Bb Aa

goat

G G G

g g g

G a A g

B f E c C

7

hamster

Name:

H H H

h h h

H h G g

F f E e

Trace and write.

bed

head

cab

bead

bag

egg

Match It Up

I I

i i

hide

I hide.

9

Name:

J J

j j

jab

I jab.

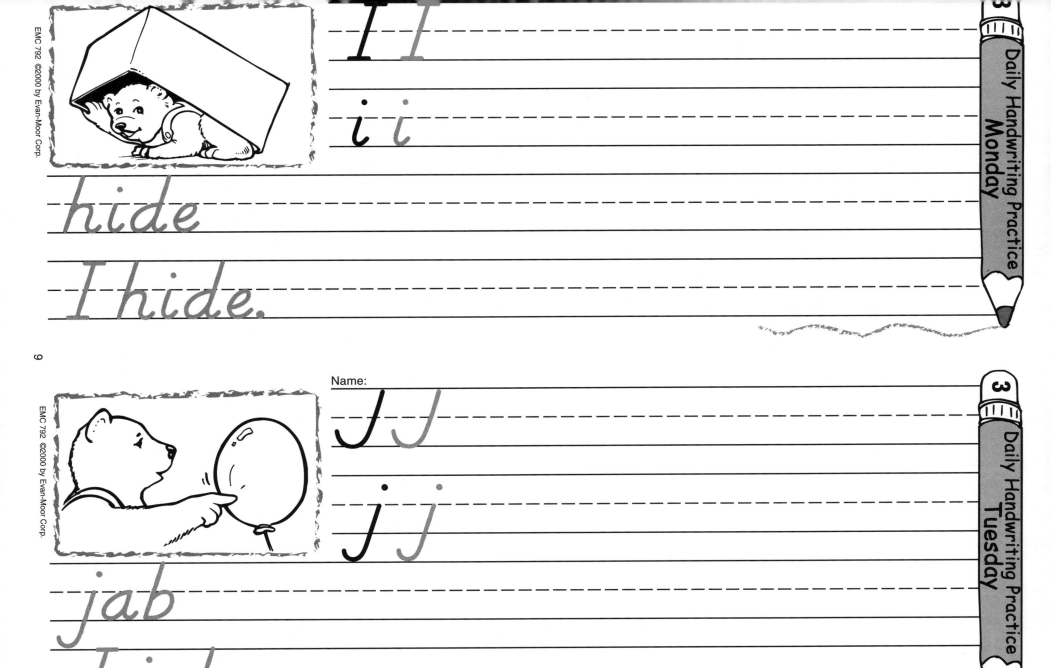

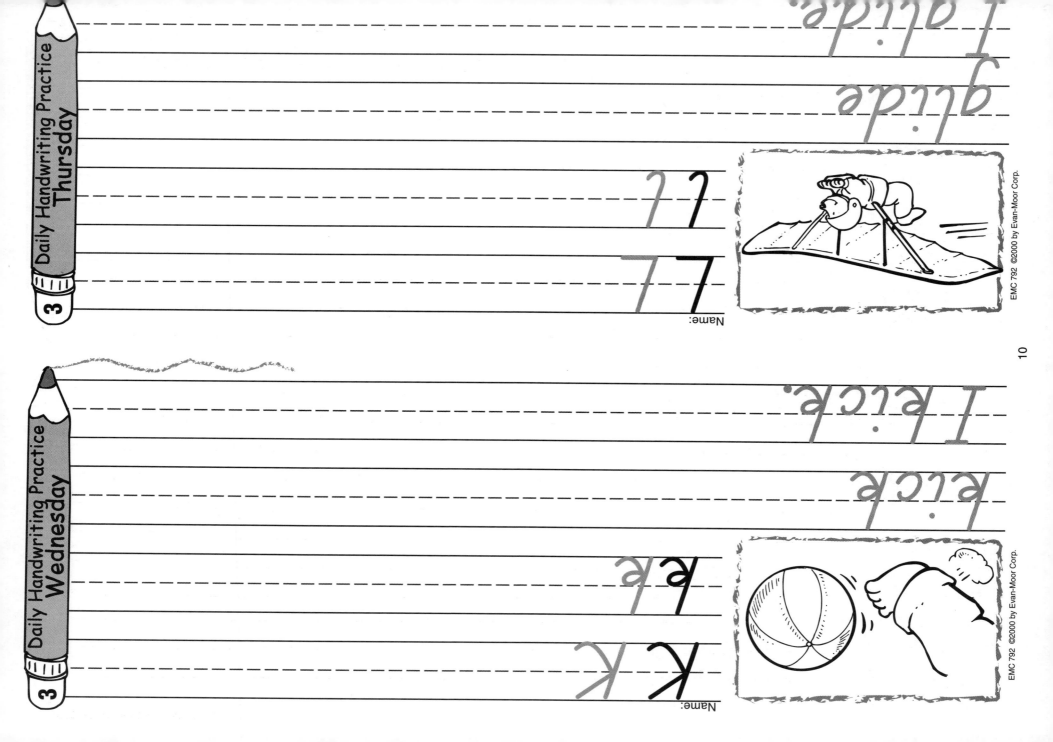

Daily Handwriting Practice
Thursday

glide

I glide

Name:

3

Daily Handwriting Practice
Wednesday

kick

I kick

Name:

Things I Can Do

Trace and write.

I hide.

I kick.

I glide.

I jab.

I lace.

I dig.

I beg.

11

Mmmm!

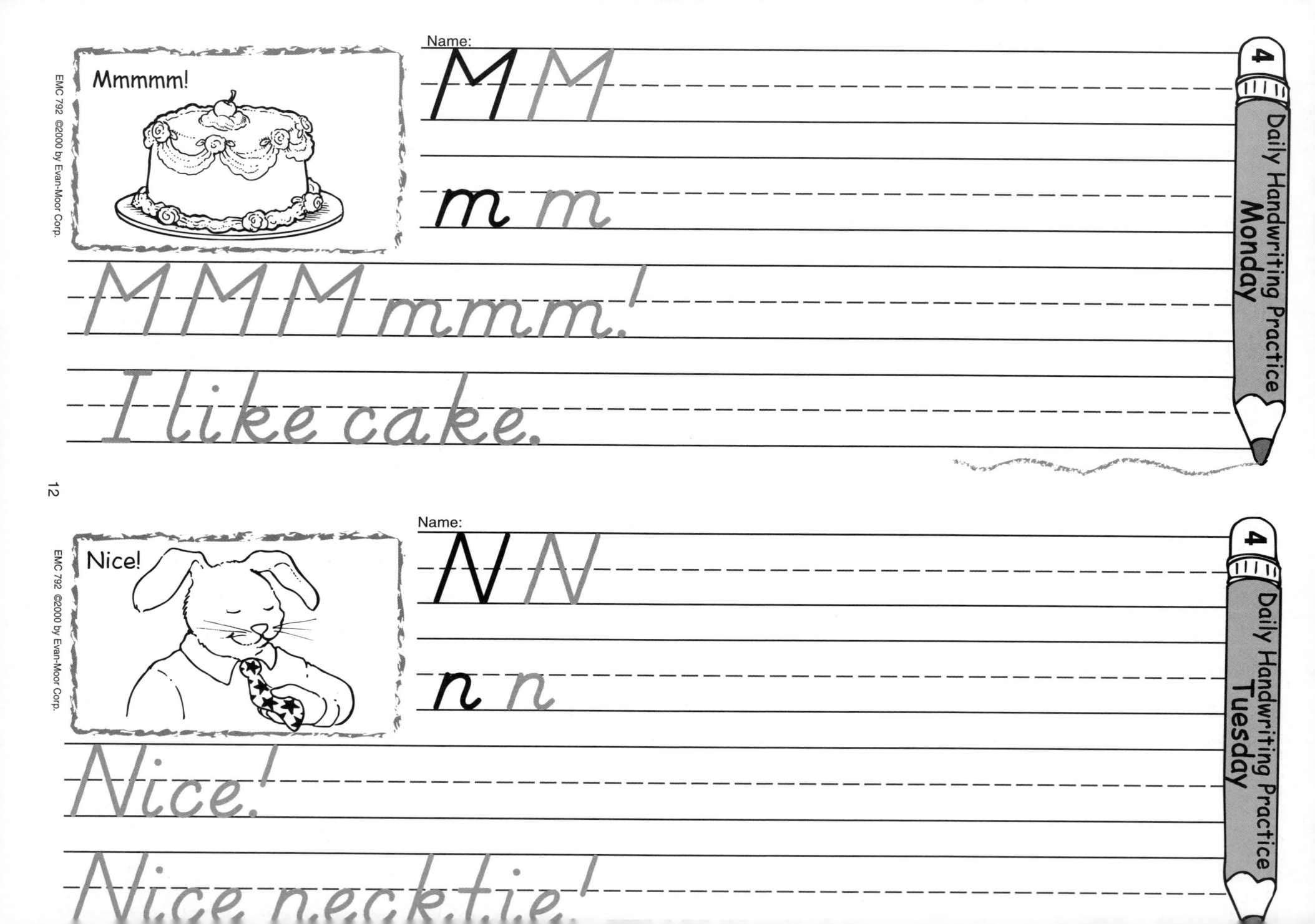

Name:

M M

m m

M M M m m m!

I like cake.

12

Nice!

Name:

N N

n n

Nice!

Nice necktie!

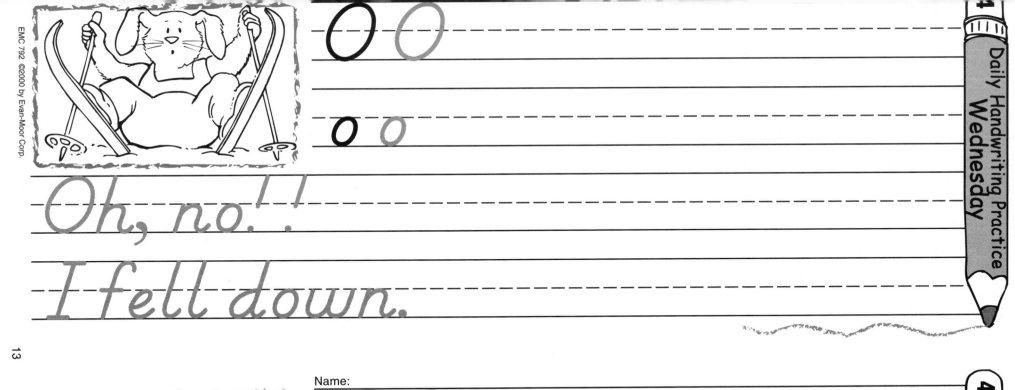

O O

o o

Oh, no!!!

I fell down.

13

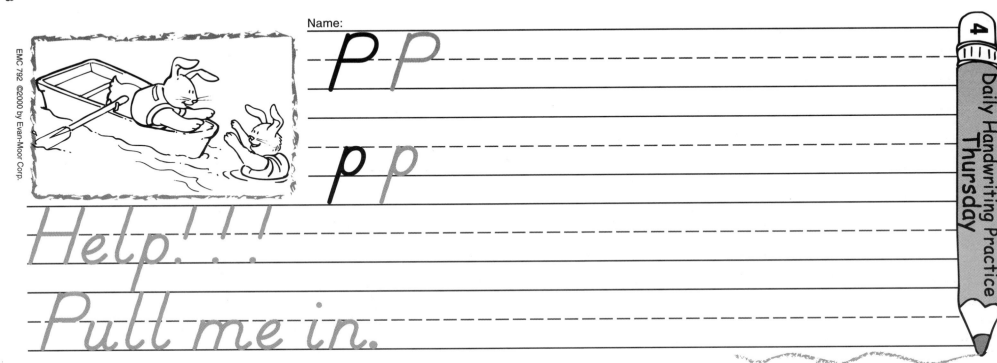

Name:

P P

P P

Help.!!!

Pull me in.

Ben Digs

Can Ben find a map?
Can Ben find a bone?

Can Ben find a map?

Dig, Ben, Dig.
Dig deep.
Find a bone.

Good job, Ben.

Q Q

q q

Qq

Qq Quack, quack.

15

Name:

R R

r r

Rr

Rr Roar. Grrrrrr!

Name:

S S

s s

Eeeee!

Ss

Scream.

16

Name:

T T

t t

Tt

Timber!

Name: _____

Trace

*Tell a tale
of a snail
in a pail.*

Write

_____
_____
_____
_____

*Make a wish
for a fish
on a dish.*

_____
_____
_____
_____

17

EMC 792 ©2000 by Evan-Moor Corp.

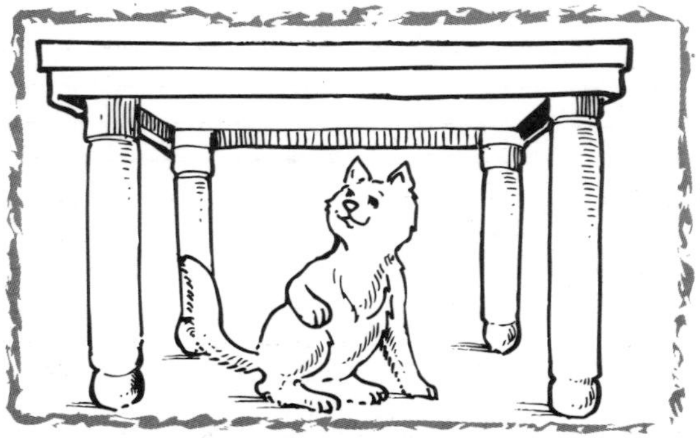

Name:

Daily Handwriting Practice
Monday
9

U U u u

under

The kitten is under the table.

Name:

Daily Handwriting Practice
Tuesday
9

V V v v

over

Swing over the river, Fido.

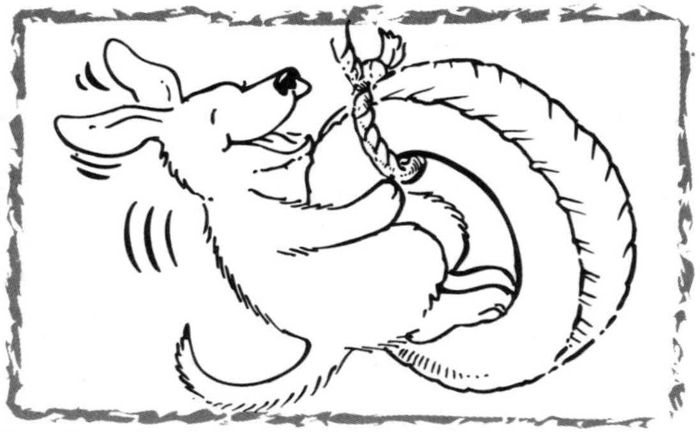

Name:

Daily Handwriting Practice
Wednesday
6

W W w w

Where

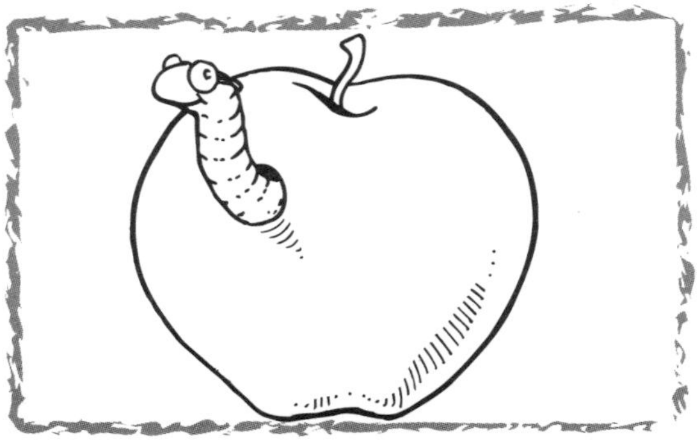

Where is Willy the worm?

Name:

Daily Handwriting Practice
Thursday
6

X X x x

Xx

X marks the spot on the map.

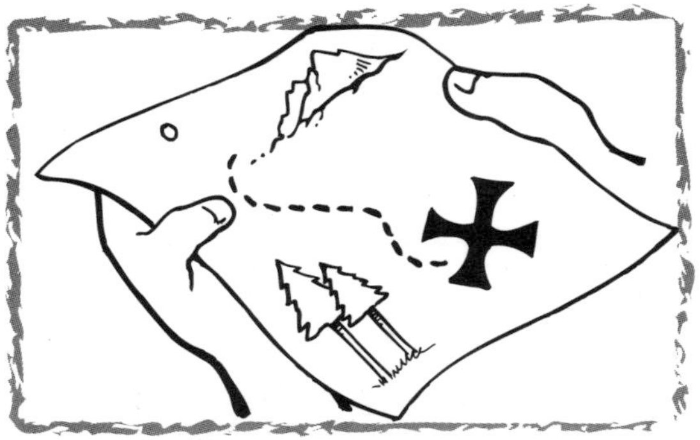

Name: _____

The glass holds 2 cups.
Excellent!

The glass holds 2 cups.

The pan holds one quart.
Excellent!

The tub holds two wet pups.
Do you have a towel?

20

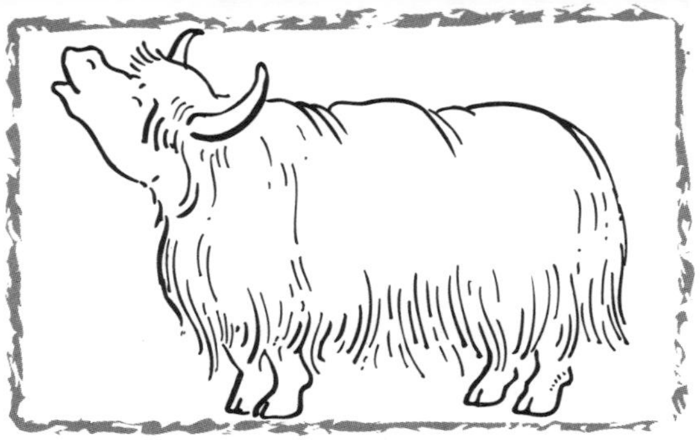

Y Y

y y

yelp yowl

yeah yank

7 Daily Handwriting Practice Monday

Name:

Z Z

z z

zip zonk

zing zoom

7 Daily Handwriting Practice Tuesday

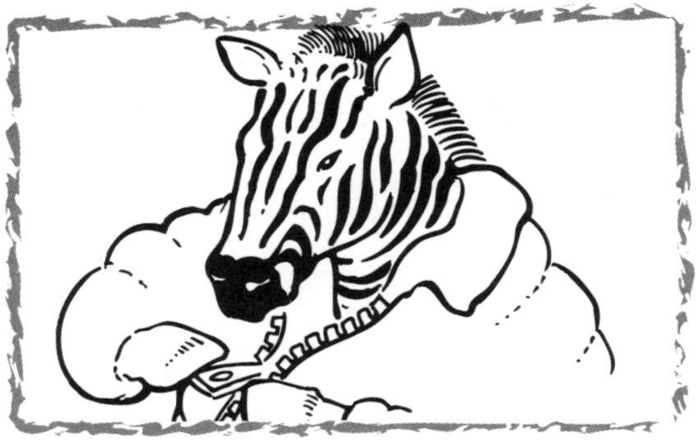

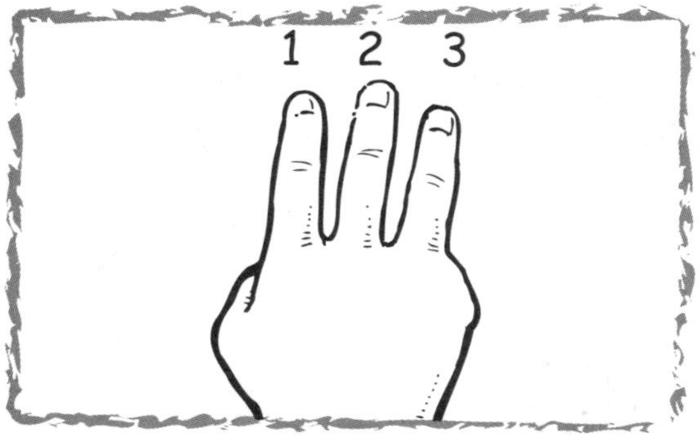

Name:

one   two

three

I can count 1, 2, 3.

22

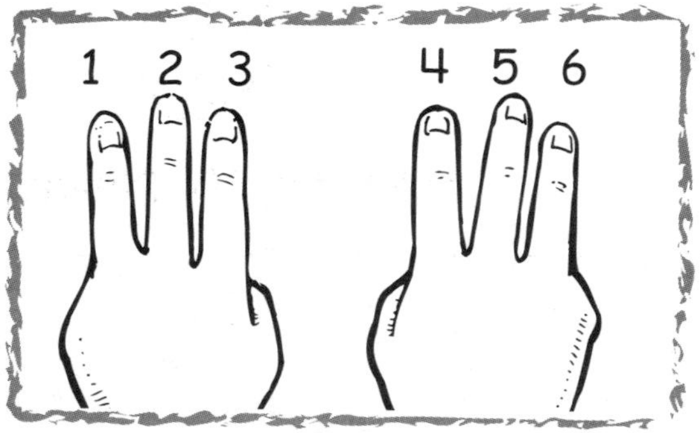

Name:

four   five

six

I can count 1, 2, 3, 4, 5, 6.

Name: _____

Trace and write.

Yes, please.

No, thank you.

Would you like some?

23

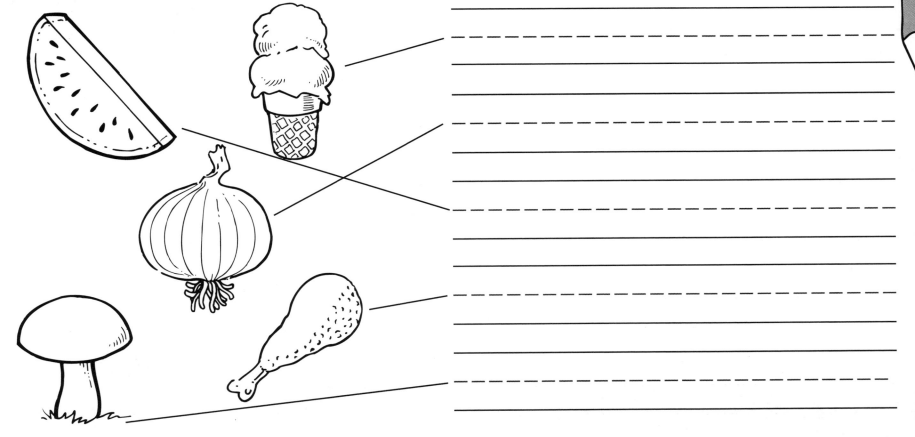

Roses are red, violets are blue.

red

r　e　d

Name:

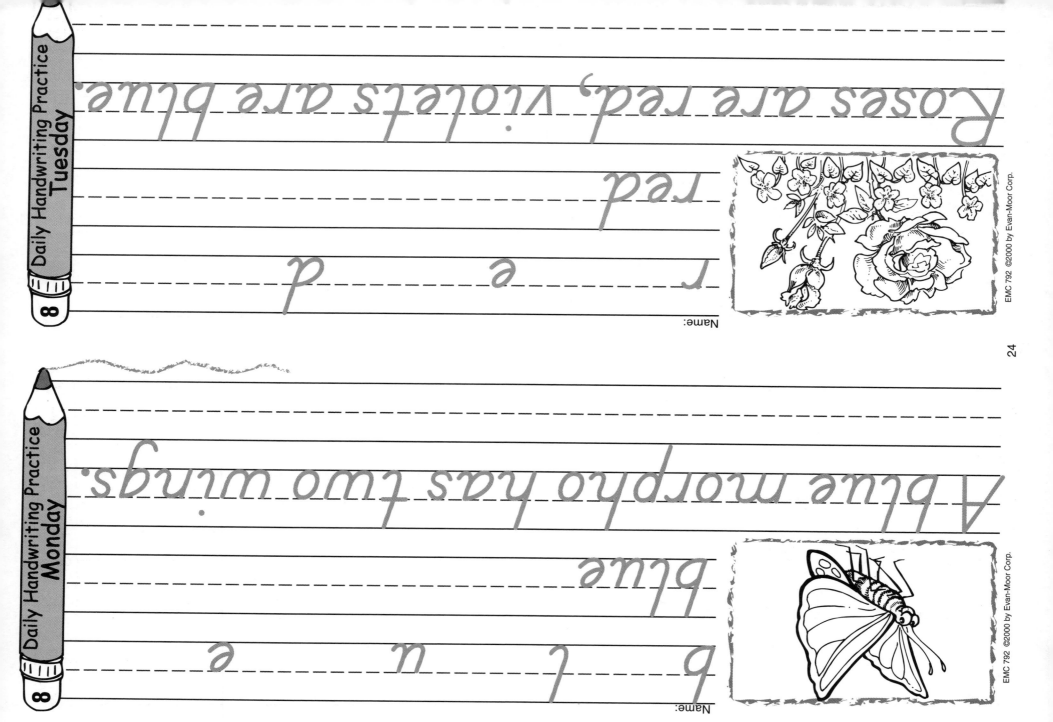

EMC 792 ©2000 by Evan-Moor Corp.

24

A blue morpho has two wings.

blue

b　l　u　e

Name:

EMC 792 ©2000 by Evan-Moor Corp.

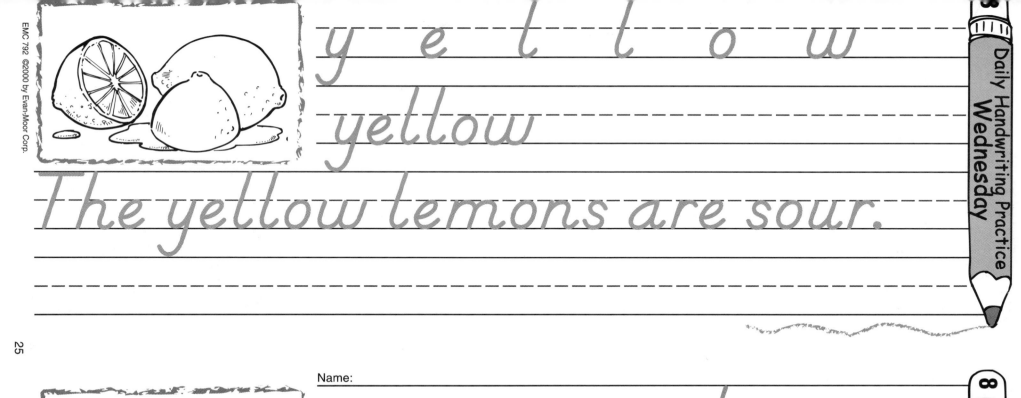

y e l l o w

yellow

The yellow lemons are sour.

EMC 792 ©2000 by Evan-Moor Corp.

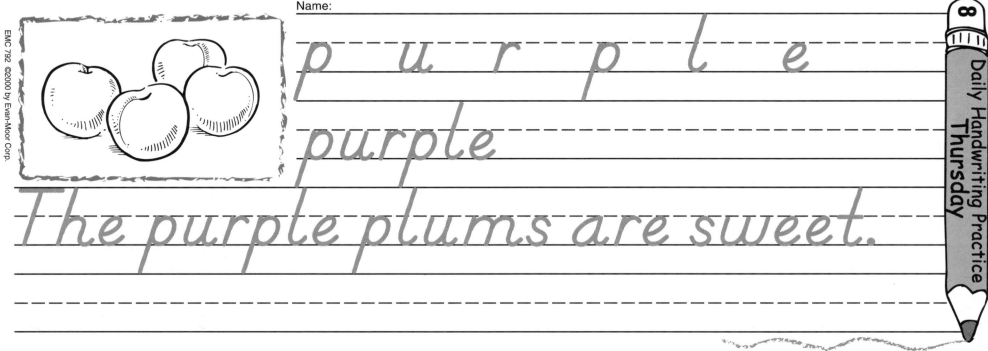

Name:

p u r p l e

purple

The purple plums are sweet.

EMC 792 ©2000 by Evan-Moor Corp.

Name: _____

Color and write.

Mister
Clown

red ○

yellow

blue

purple

26

The clown's hat is _____.

_____

The clown's tie is _____.

_____

The clown's nose is _____.

_____

The clown's hair is _____.

_____

g r e e n

green

Green grass tickles my toes.

Name:

o r a n g e

orange

I picked an orange pumpkin.

9

Brown bear, what do you see?

brown

b r o w n

Name:

EMC 792 ©2000 by Evan-Moor Corp.

28

The pink piglets are cute.

pink

p i n k

Name:

EMC 792 ©2000 by Evan-Moor Corp.

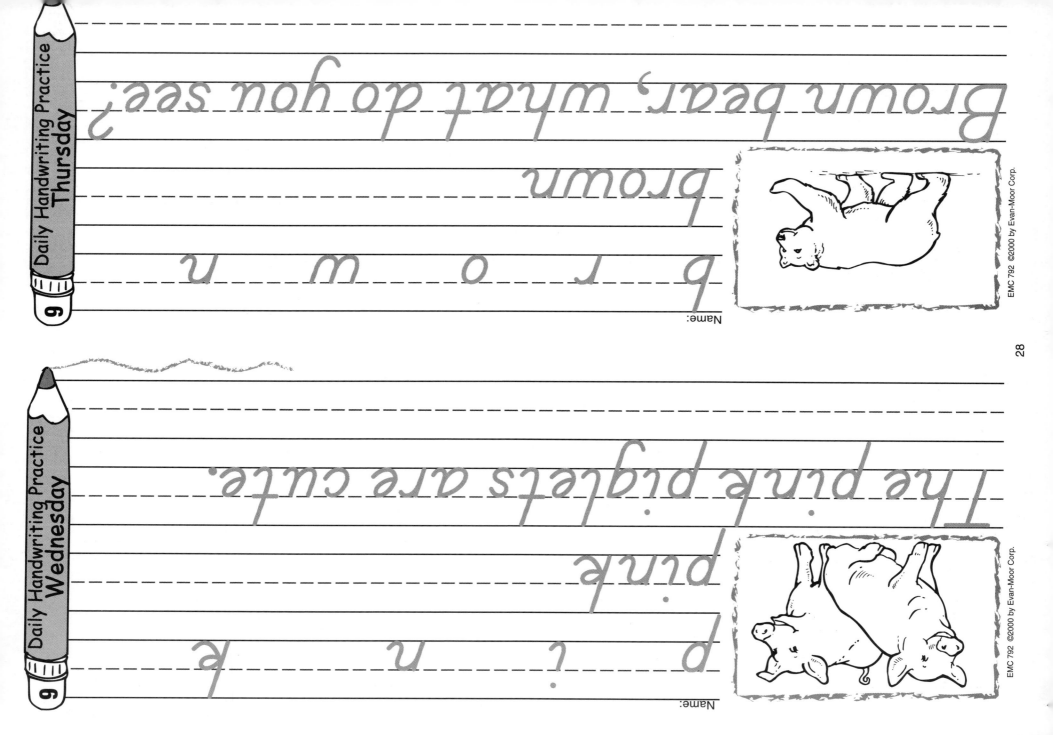

Name: _____

The Color Wheel

red

blue   yellow

red   orange   yellow   green   blue   purple

29

Color and copy.

Red and blue make purple.

_____

- -

Blue and yellow make green.

_____

- -

Yellow and red make orange.

_____

- -

_____

EMC 792 ©2000 by Evan-Moor Corp.

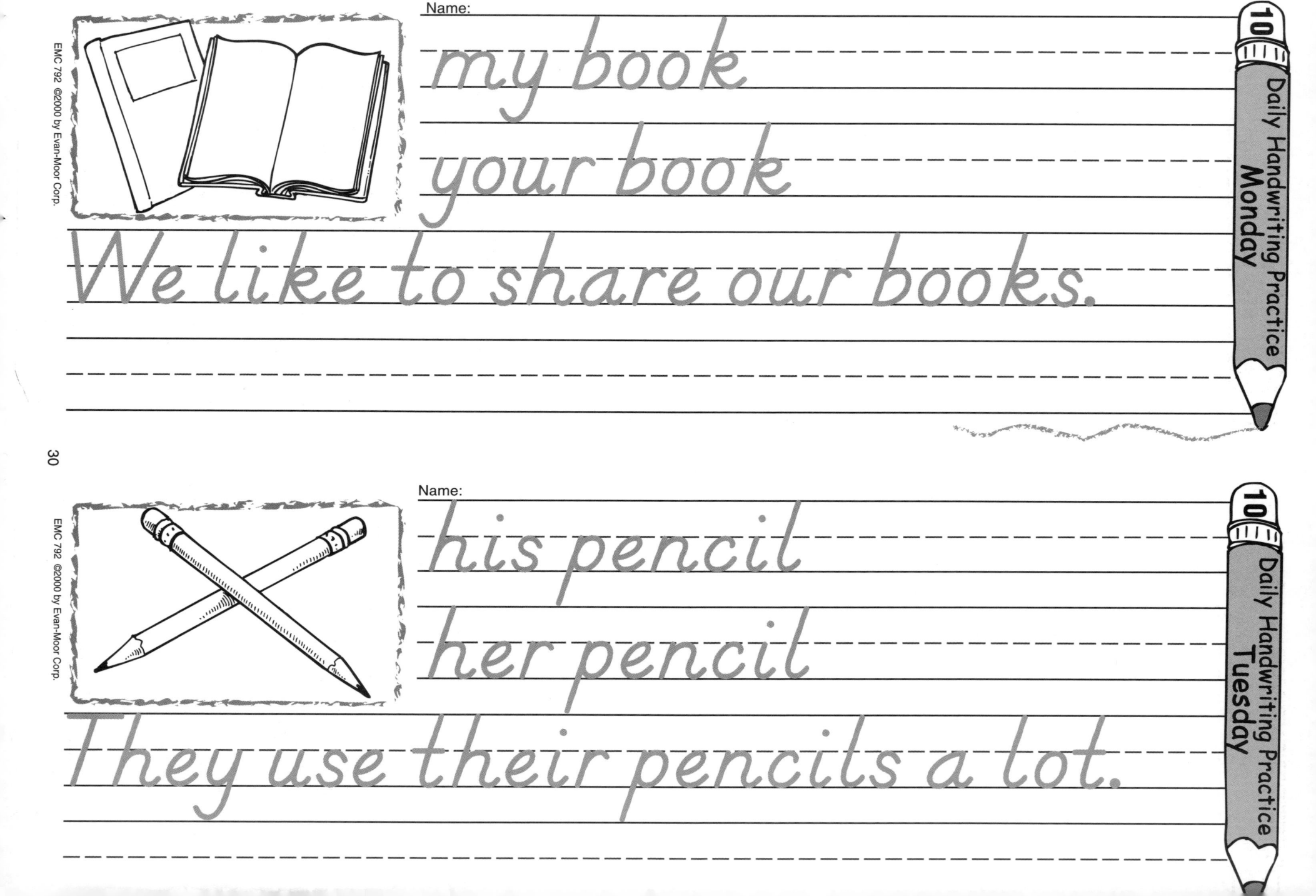

Name:

my book

your book

We like to share our books.

30

Name:

his pencil

her pencil

They use their pencils a lot.

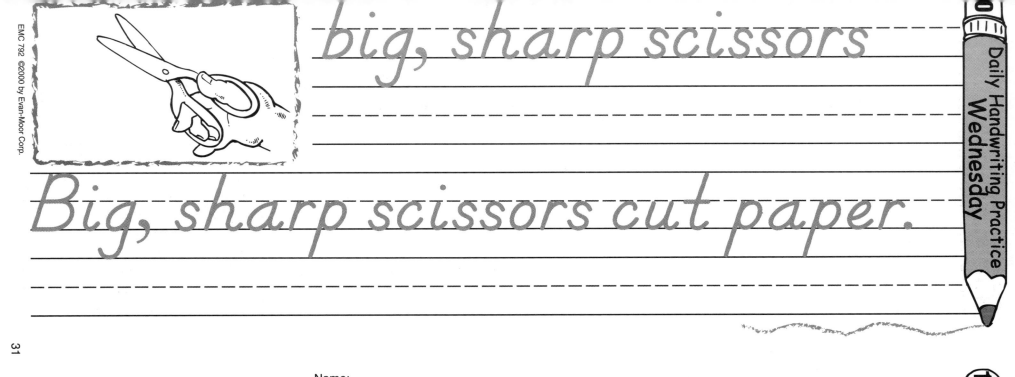

big, sharp scissors

Big, sharp scissors cut paper.

31

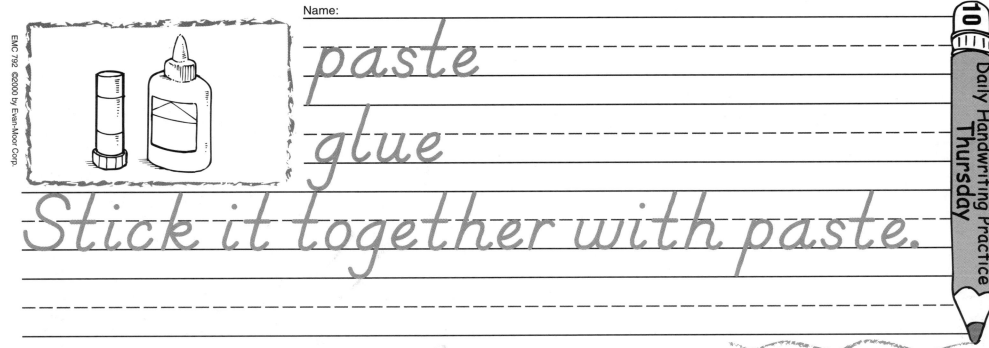

Name:

paste

glue

Stick it together with paste.

Name: _____

At School

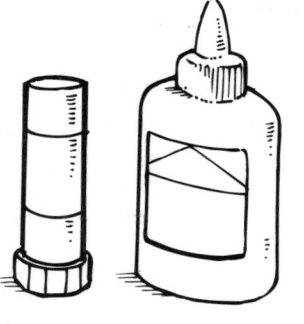

We use tools to help us at school.

We use scissors to cut.

We use pencils to write.

We use glue and paste to stick things together.

Copy the story.

32

skip

rope

Muff loves to run and jump.

33

Name:

kick

score

Mac will catch the football.

Name:

Good for you.

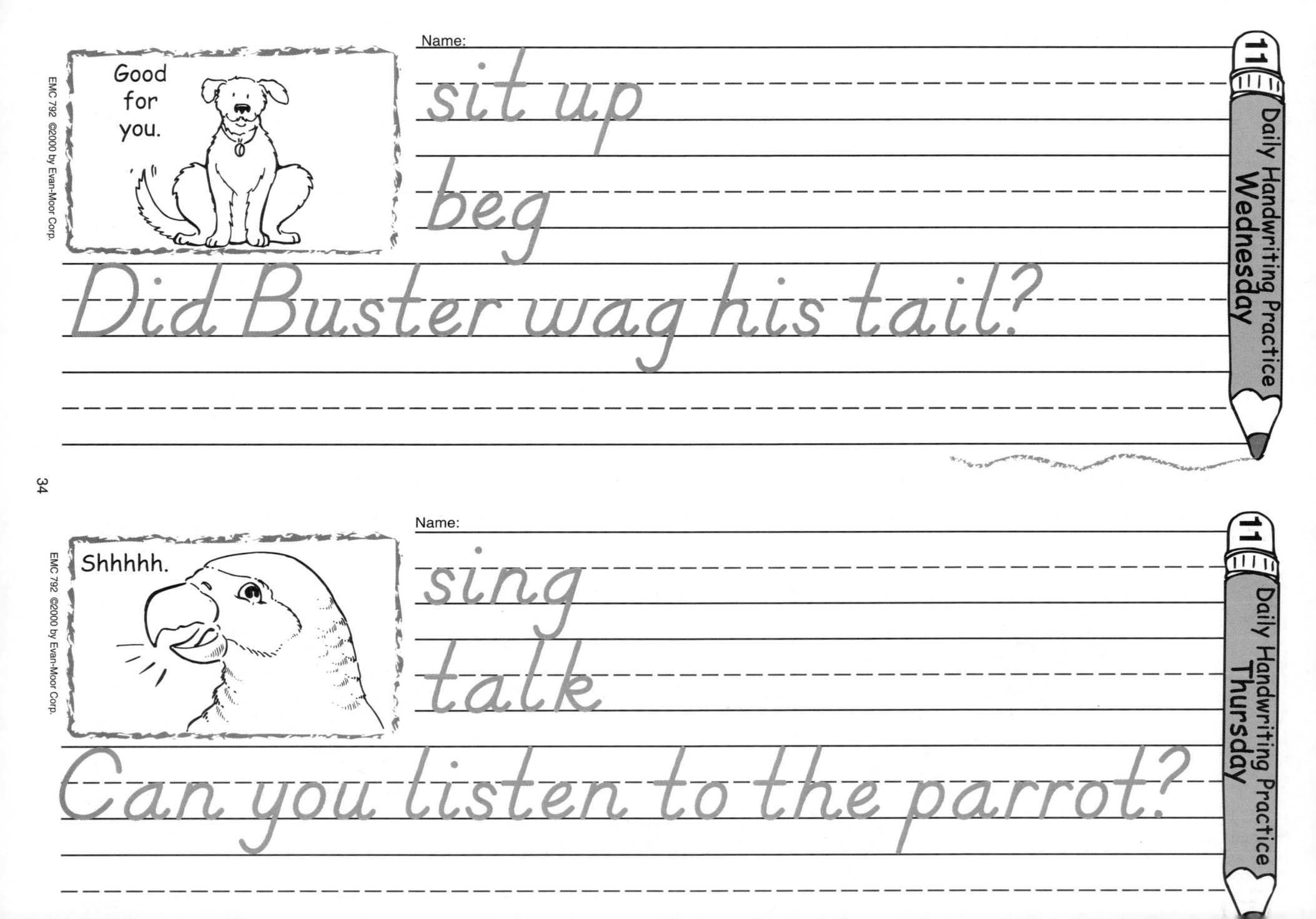

sit up

beg

Did Buster wag his tail?

34

Name:

Shhhhh.

sing

talk

Can you listen to the parrot?

Name: _____

Frogs Hop

We go fast and we go slow.

Watch and see how fast we go.

Run and jump and skip and hop.

We go fast and never stop.

Copy the poem.

_____

- -

_____

_____

_____

_____

- -

_____

- -

_____

EMC 792 ©2000 by Evan-Moor Corp.

EMC 792 ©2000 by Evan-Moor Corp.

toast

cereal

I eat a balanced breakfast.

36

EMC 792 ©2000 by Evan-Moor Corp.

soup

sandwich

I eat a nutritious lunch.

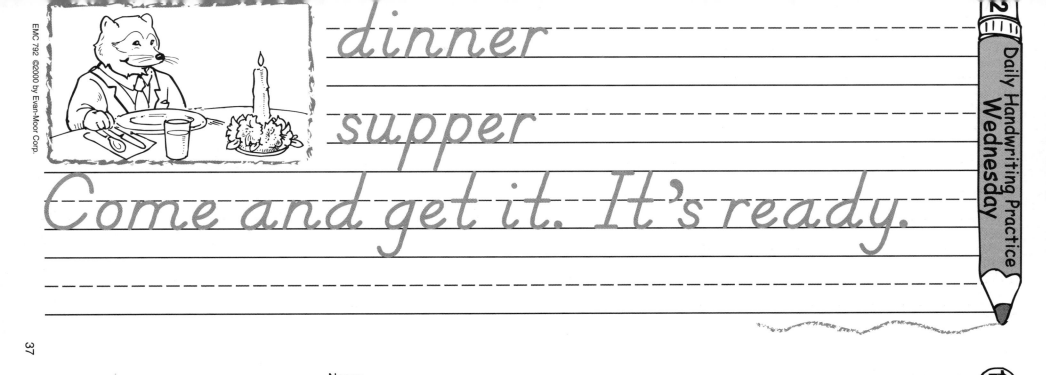

dinner

supper

Come and get it. It's ready.

Name:

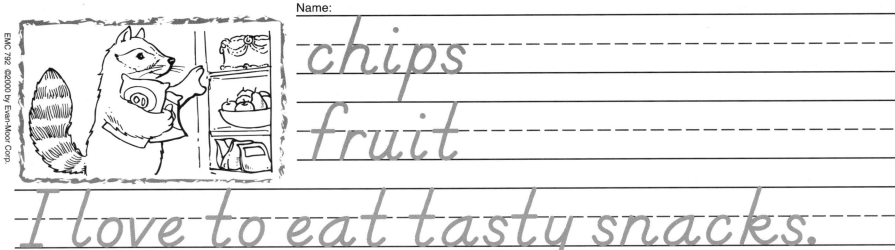

chips

fruit

I love to eat tasty snacks.

Name: _____

Lettuce Roll-up

Wash one lettuce leaf.
Spread peanut butter on it.
Sprinkle with raisins.
Roll up the leaf.
Eat and enjoy.

Copy the recipe.

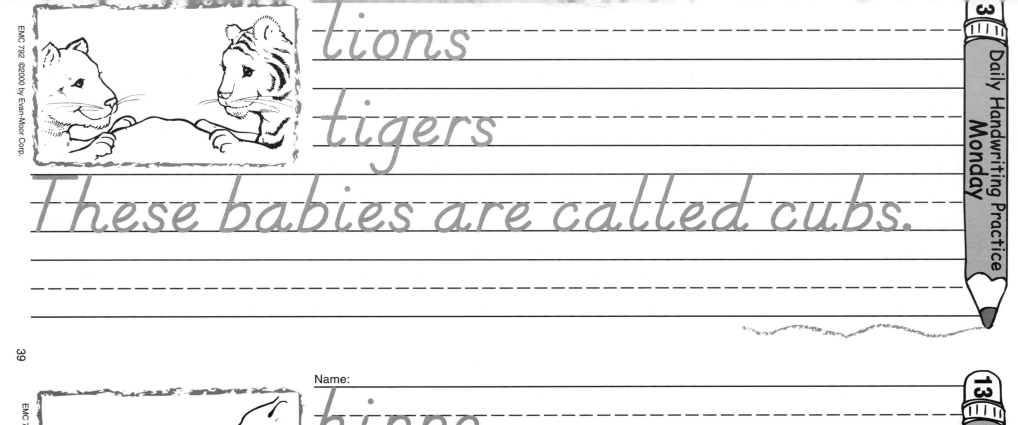

lions

tigers

These babies are called cubs.

Name:

hippo

elephant

These animals like water.

These animals have big horns.

antelope

addax

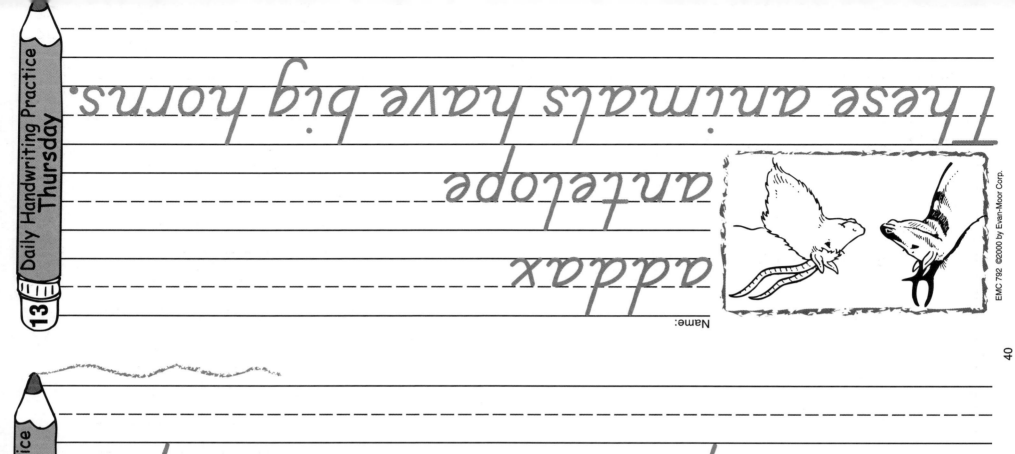

EMC 792 ©2000 by Evan-Moor Corp.

One has spots. One has stripes.

giraffe

zebra

EMC 792 ©2000 by Evan-Moor Corp.

Name: _____

Name the animal.

Welcome to the Zoo
hippo
elephant
lion
tiger
addax
antelope
giraffe
zebra

41

Name:

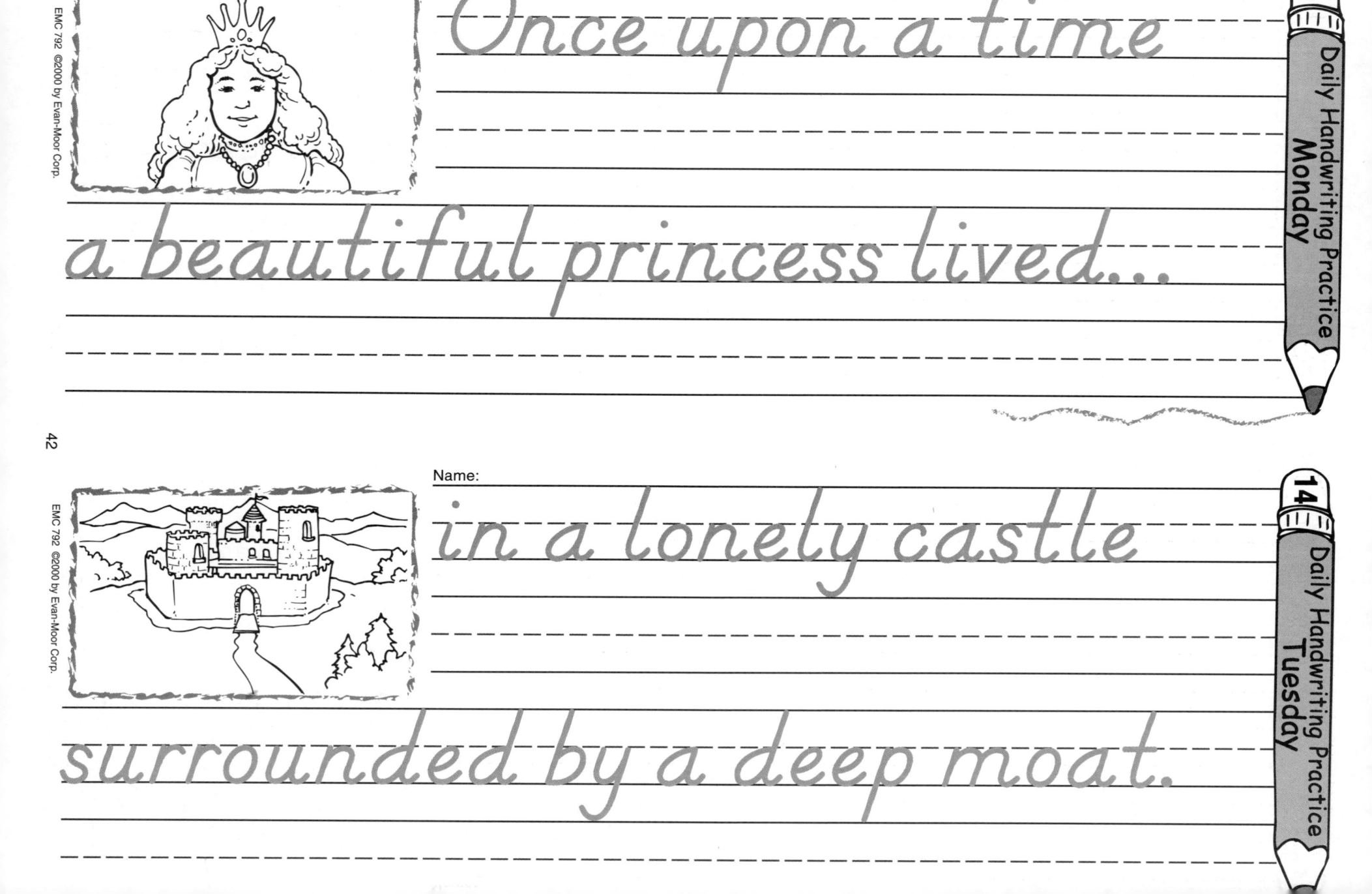

Once upon a time

a beautiful princess lived...

42

Name:

in a lonely castle

surrounded by a deep moat.

Name:

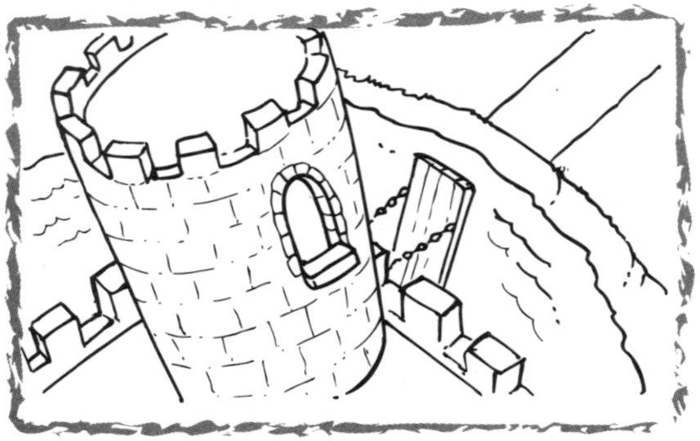

She sat in the tower

and wished she had a friend.

14 Daily Handwriting Practice Wednesday

Name:

She was very sad.

Would she ever find a friend?

14 Daily Handwriting Practice Thursday

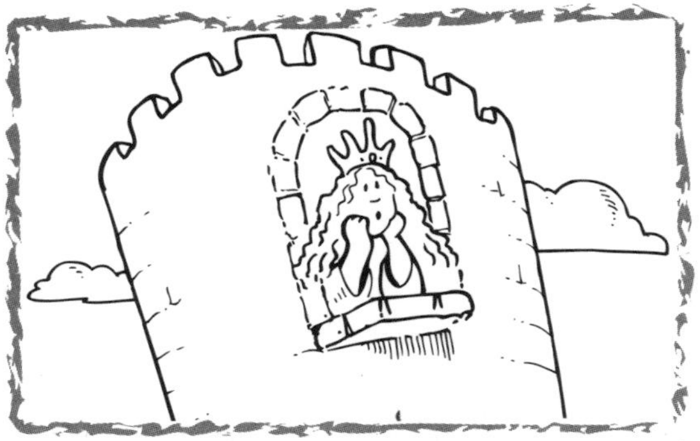

Name: _____

The Princess

Once upon a time there was a beautiful princess. She lived in a castle with a moat. She had no visitors. She was lonely.

Finish the story.

_____

- -

_____

- -

_____

- -

_____

- -

Word Box

handsome prince

snuggly kitten

happily ever after

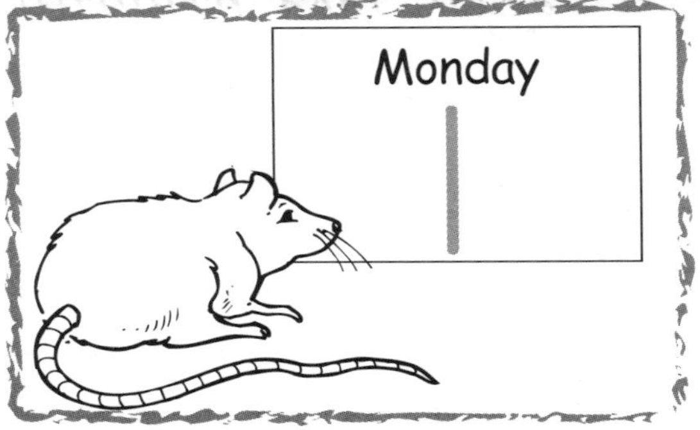

Monday
1

Monday

Monday

Today is marvelous Monday.

45

Name:

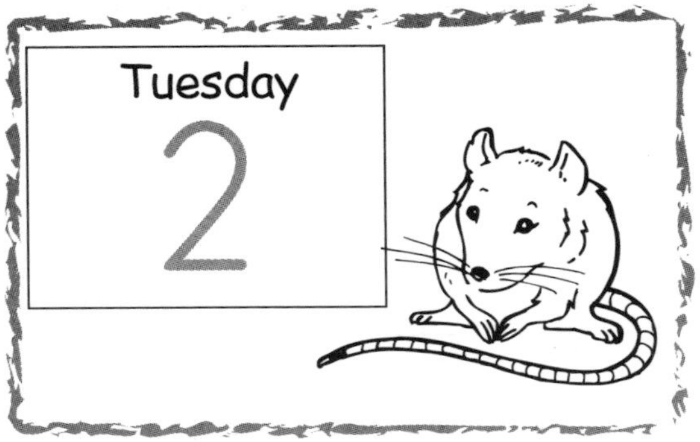

Tuesday
2

Tuesday

Tuesday

Today is terrific Tuesday.

Wednesday
3

Name:

Wednesday

Today is wacky Wednesday.

46

Thursday
4

Name:

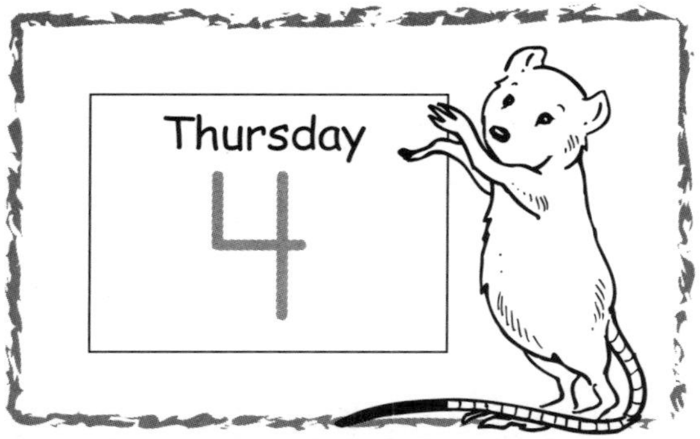

Thursday

Thursday

Today is thrilling Thursday.

Name: _____

What a Week!

Today is Friday.
Finally, a fun-filled Friday.
We had a marvelous Monday,
a terrific Tuesday,
a wacky Wednesday,
and a thrilling Thursday.

Read and copy.

Today is Friday.

What kind of pizza do you like?

Name:

veggie

cheese

pepperoni

I like

48

What kind of sandwich do you like?

Name:

ham

tuna

peanut butter

I like

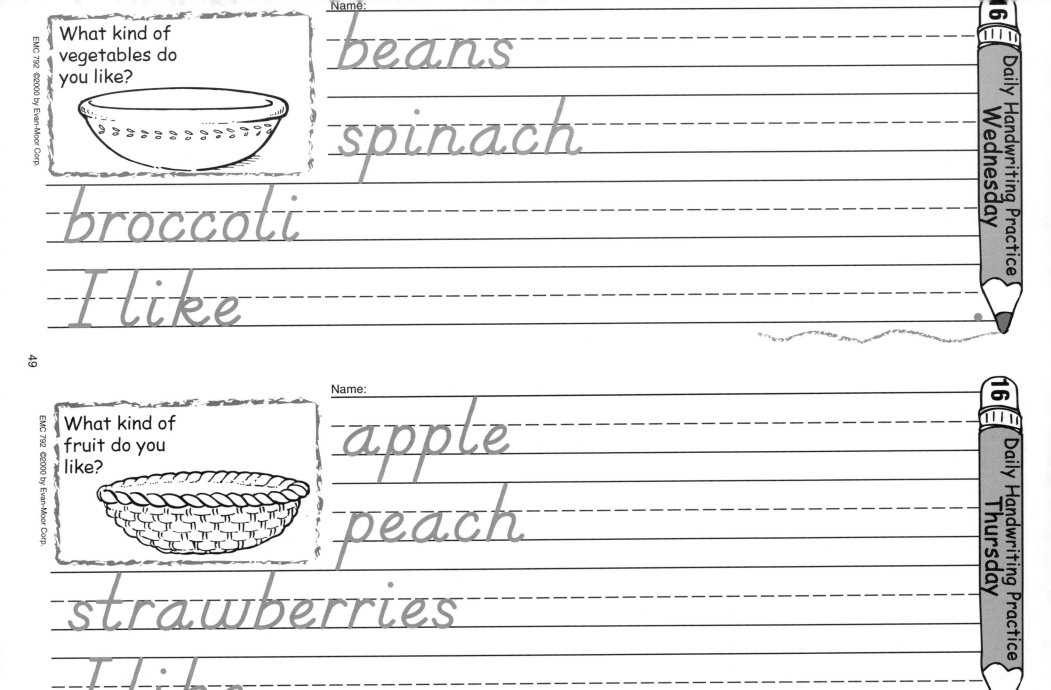

What kind of vegetables do you like?

EMC 792 ©2000 by Evan-Moor Corp.

beans

spinach

broccoli

I like

49

What kind of fruit do you like?

EMC 792 ©2000 by Evan-Moor Corp.

Name:

apple

peach

strawberries

I like

Cooking

Copy this poem.

50

Measure and pour.
Stir it to mix.
Look at the things
That I can fix.

Pudding, pretzels
Sandwiches, too.
I think it's fun
To cook for you.

Name:

There were **five** in the nest
When there came a request.
Move over! Move over!
So the **five** moved over
And one fell out.

five   four

Move over!

Five minus one equals four.

51

Name:

There were **four** in the nest
When there came a request.
Move over! Move over!
So the **four** moved over
And one fell out.

four   three

Move over!

Four minus one equals three.

EMC 792 ©2000 by Evan-Moor Corp.

There were **three** in the nest
When there came a request.
Move over! Move over!
So the **three** moved over
And one fell out.

Name:

three   *two*

Move over!

Three minus one equals two.

52

EMC 792 ©2000 by Evan-Moor Corp.

There were **two** in the nest
When there came a request.
Move over! Move over!
So the **two** moved over
And one fell out.

Name:

two   *one*

Move over!

Two minus one equals one.

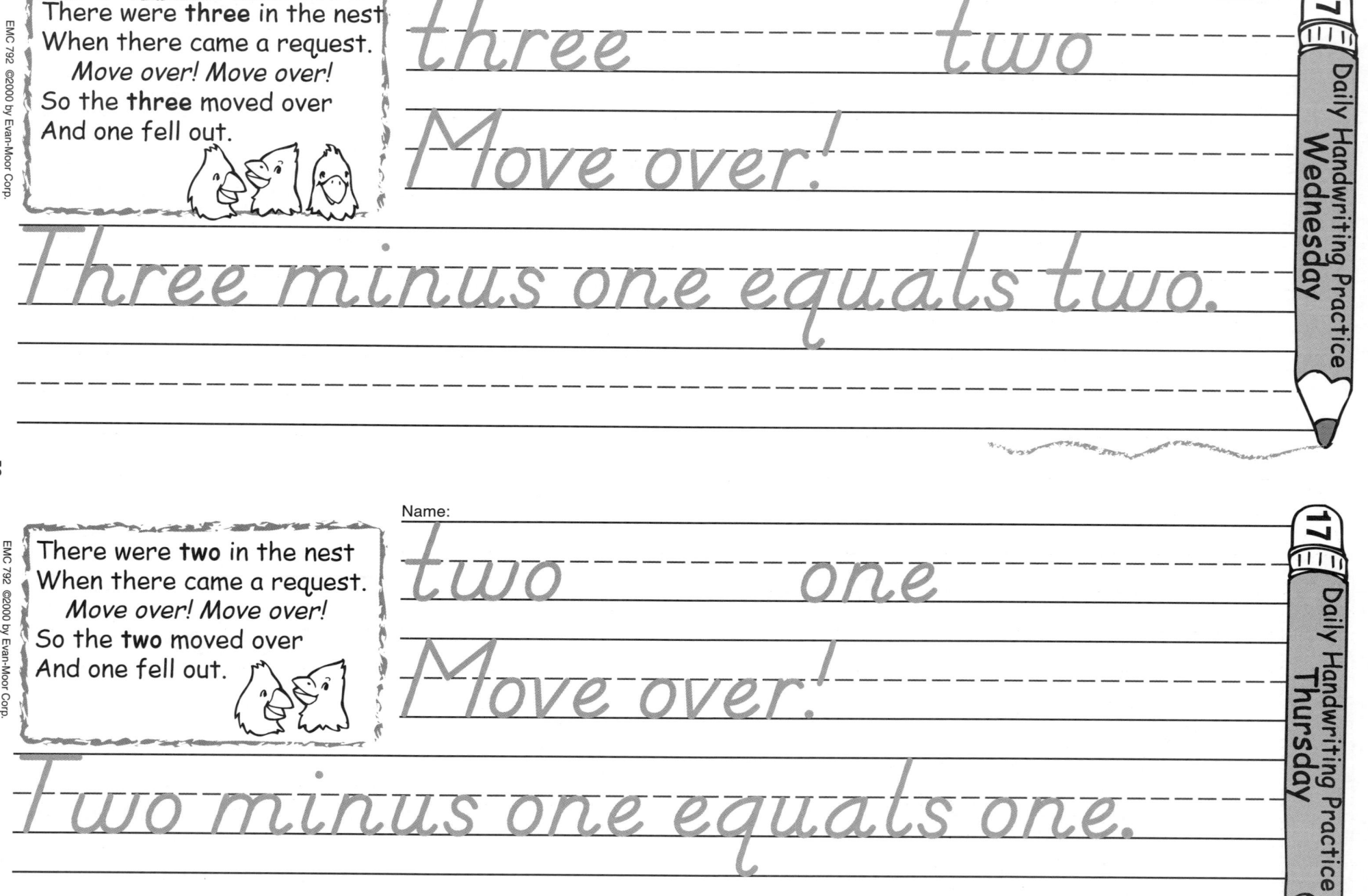

Trace and write the numbers.

There was **one** in the nest
And, at last, no request.
Just a quiet time for rest.
Shhhhhh.

five

four

three

two

one

Sweet dreams.

Sleep tight.

EMC 792 ©2000 by Evan-Moor Corp.

Name:

curves

corners

Shapes have curves or corners.

54

Name:

circle

square

triangle

Name the shapes.

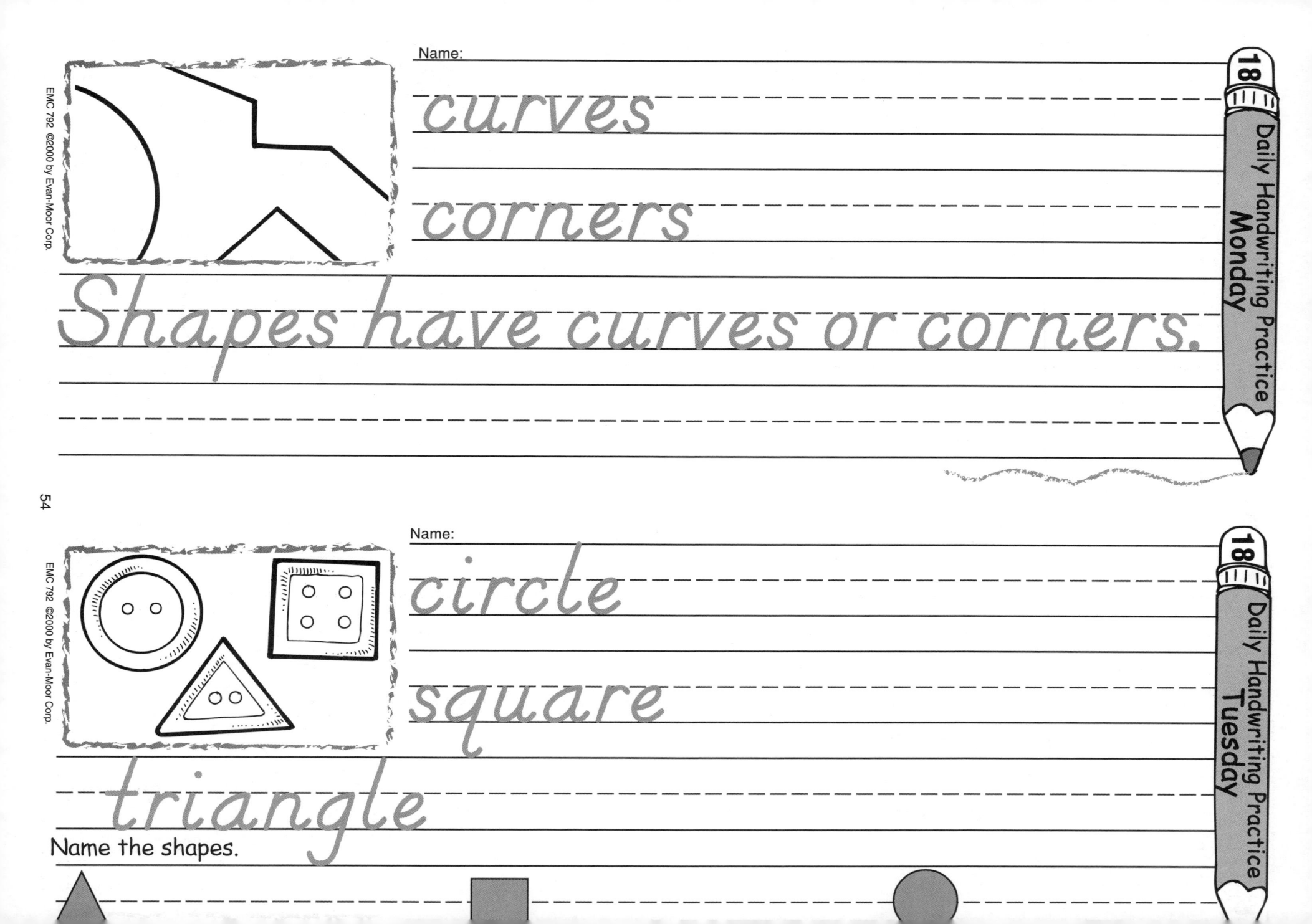

8

EMC 792 ©2000 by Evan-Moor Corp.

pentagon

octagon

rectangle

Name the shapes.

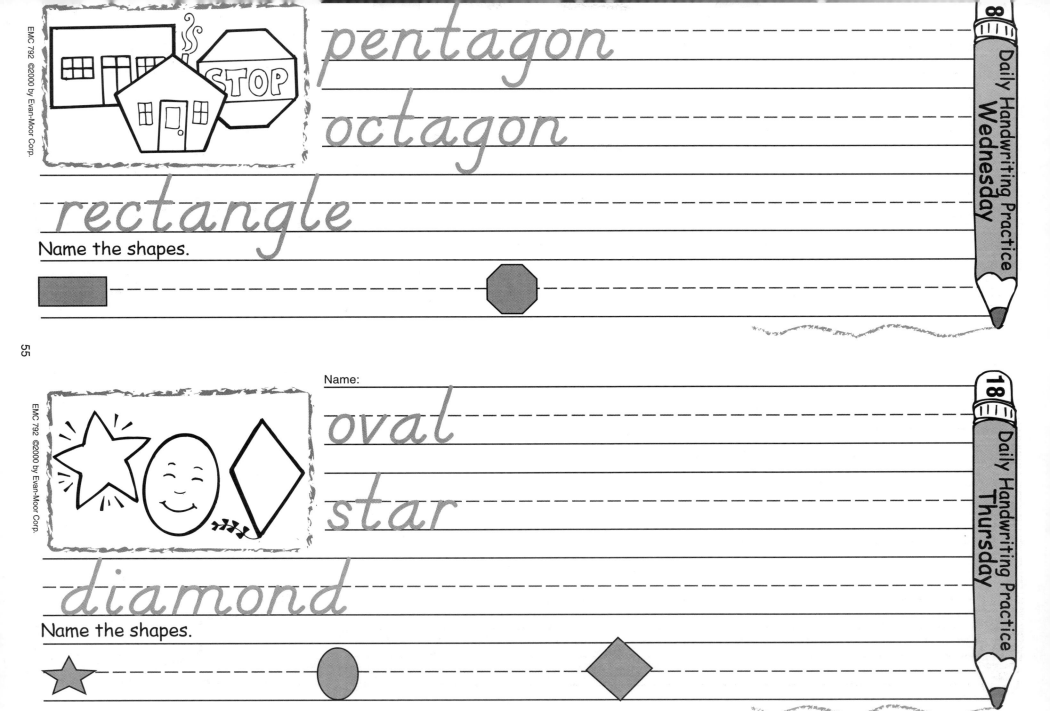

Name:

EMC 792 ©2000 by Evan-Moor Corp.

oval

star

diamond

Name the shapes.

Name: _____

Draw a square head.

Add a rectangle body.

Make two arms and legs.

Draw a funny face on it.

Draw a triangle for a hat.

Trace and finish the picture.

Copy the directions.

What did you make?

a r

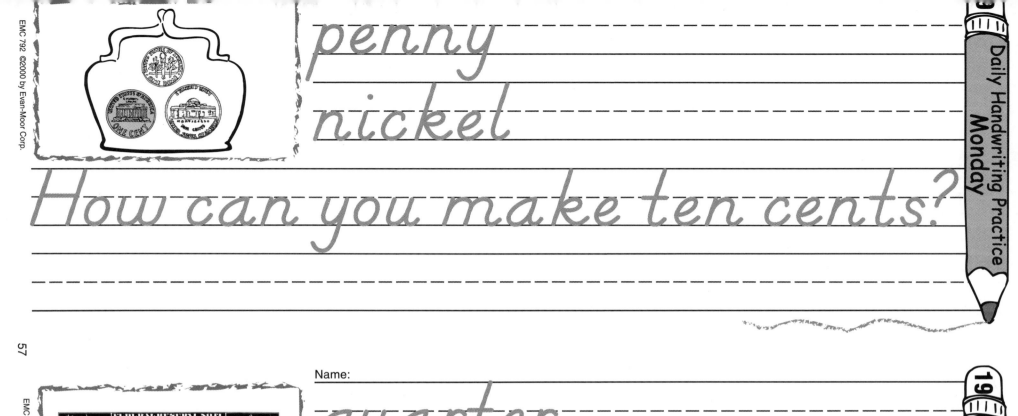

penny

nickel

How can you make ten cents?

57

Name:

quarter

dollar

Four quarters equal a dollar.

19 Daily Handwriting Practice
Thursday

Put your coins in the bank.

change

coins

Name:

EMC 792 ©2000 by Evan-Moor Corp.

19 Daily Handwriting Practice
Wednesday

I carry my bills in a wallet.

bills

dollar

Name:

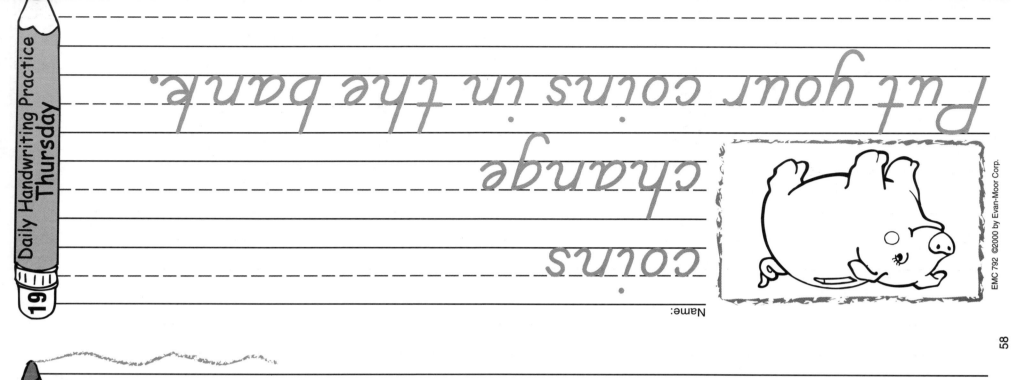

EMC 792 ©2000 by Evan-Moor Corp.

58

Money

Mom keeps her money in a purse.
Dad keeps his money in his pocket.
Granny keeps her money in a pouch.
Buster keeps his money in a bank.

Copy the sentences.

_____

_____

_____

_____

_____

_____

_____

Where do you keep your money?

_____

_____

_____

_____

Name:

The gray ant is in third place.

third

fourth

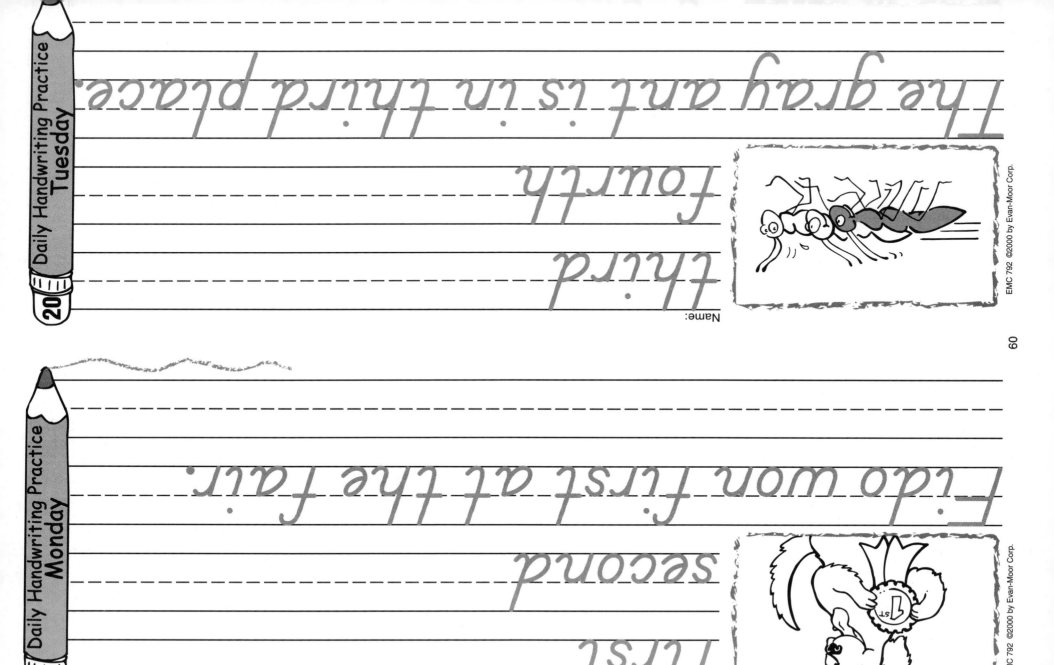

EMC 792 ©2000 by Evan-Moor Corp.

60

Name:

Ido won first at the fair.

first

second

EMC 792 ©2000 by Evan-Moor Corp.

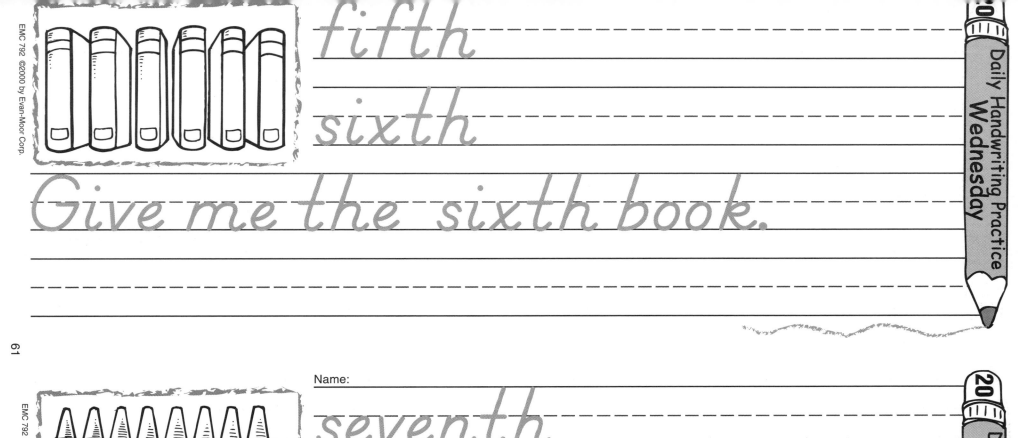

fifth

sixth

Give me the sixth book.

61

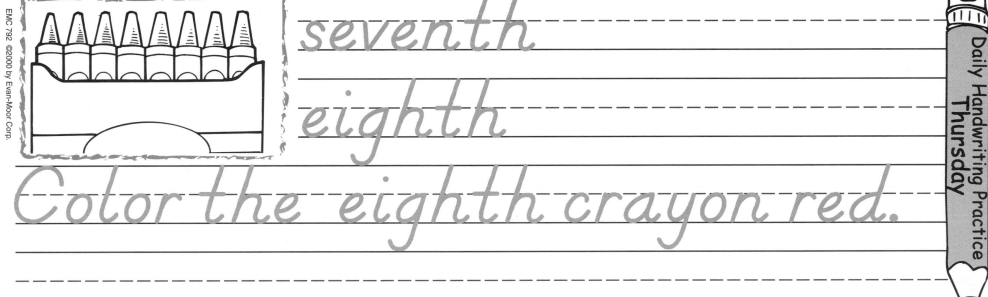

Name:

seventh

eighth

Color the eighth crayon red.

Daily Handwriting Practice
Friday
20

Write the words
to tell the order.

Name: _____

first   _fifth_

second   _sixth_

third   _seventh_

fourth   _eighth_

up

down

The flag goes up and down.

63

Name:

over

under

The birds flew over and under.

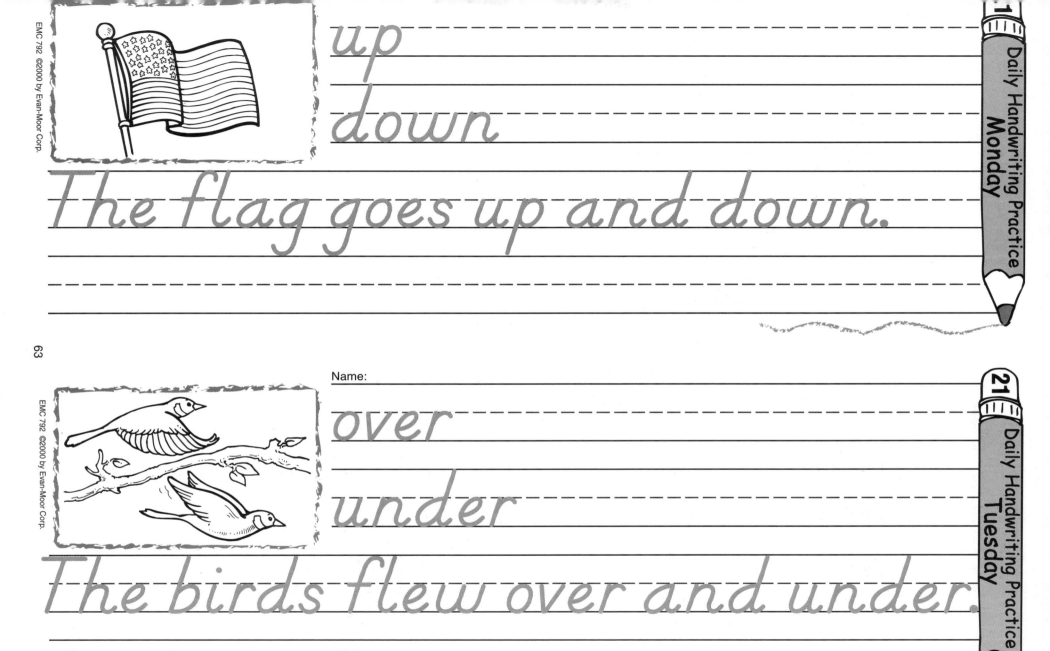

above

below

One is above. One is below.

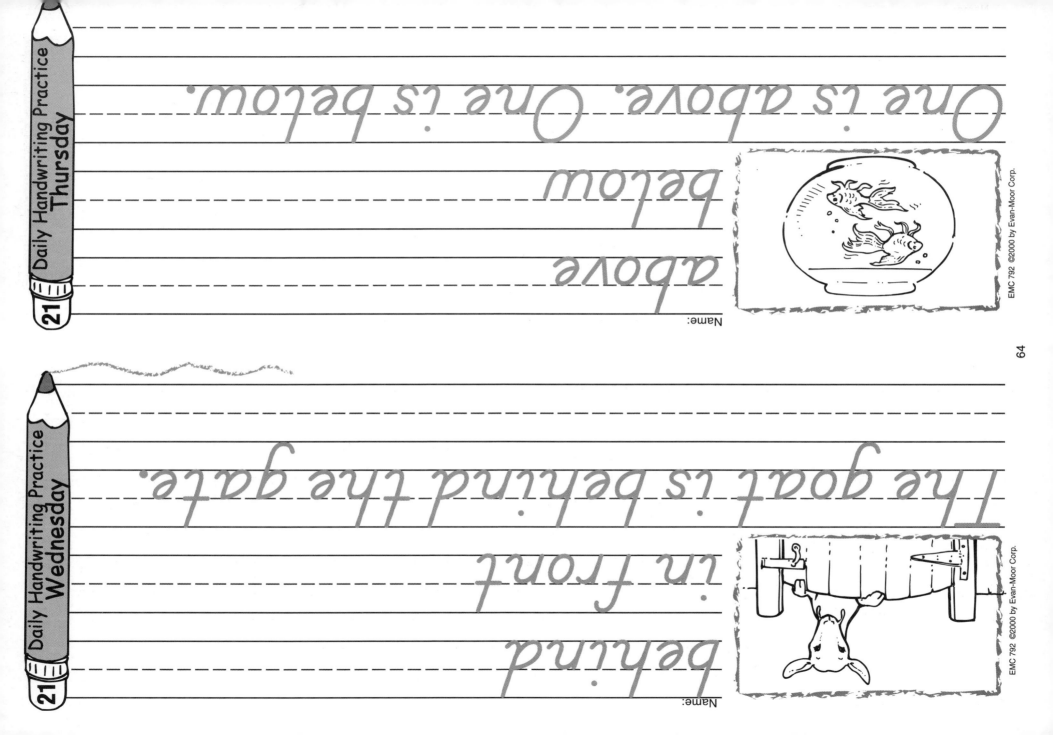

EMC 792 ©2000 by Evan-Moor Corp.

64

behind

in front

The goat is behind the gate.

EMC 792 ©2000 by Evan-Moor Corp.

Name: _____

Singing in the Rain

Match the opposites.

up	behind
in front of	under
over	below
above	down

Copy the sentences to tell about the picture.

65

The bird is above the mushroom.

_____

The mouse is below the mushroom.

_____

The fence is behind the mushroom.

_____

The leaf is in front of the mushroom.

_____

Name:

22 Daily Handwriting Practice
Monday

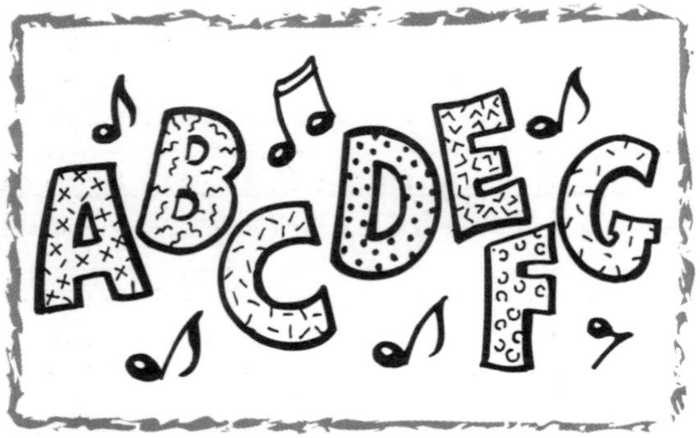

alphabetical order

Carlo, Amy, Deb, Bert, Evan

Write the names in ABC order.

Name:

22 Daily Handwriting Practice
Tuesday

I know ABC order.

Joe, Hank, Kent, Lian, Fran

Write the names in ABC order.

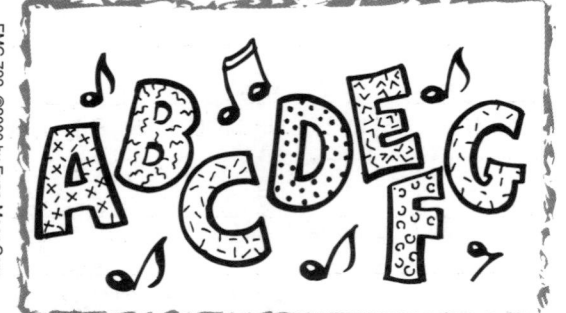

I use ABC order.

Rosa, Peg, Olaf, Said, Quon

Write the names in ABC order.

67

Name:

At the end is x, y, z.

Zach, Tala, Will, Vicki, Uri

Write the names in ABC order.

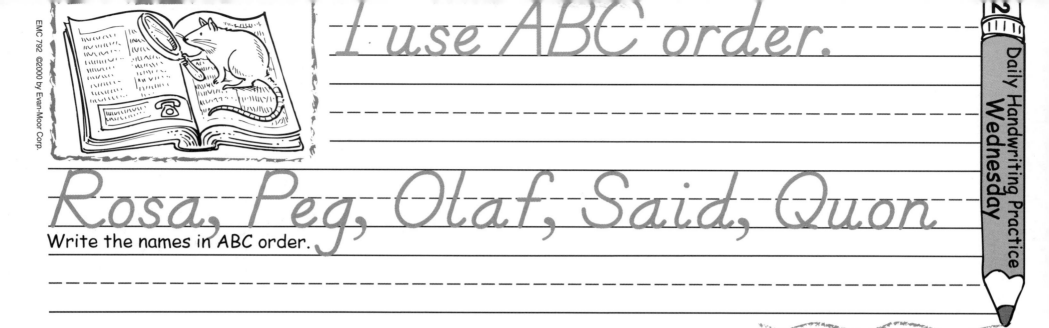

Write the letters of the alphabet.

A a

C c

N n

W w

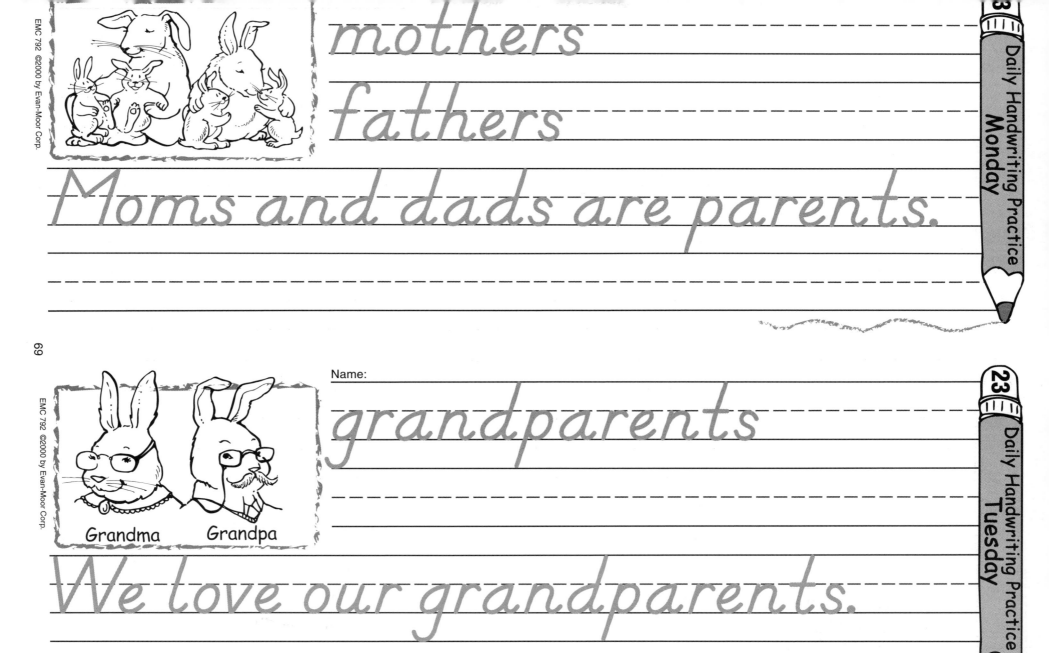

EMC 792 ©2000 by Evan-Moor Corp.

mothers

fathers

Moms and dads are parents.

EMC 792 ©2000 by Evan-Moor Corp.

Grandma   Grandpa

Name:

grandparents

We love our grandparents.

Name:

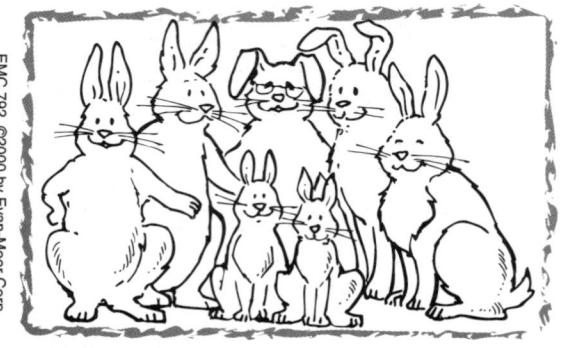

uncles

aunts

Uncles and aunts visit us.

23 Daily Handwriting Practice Wednesday

Name:

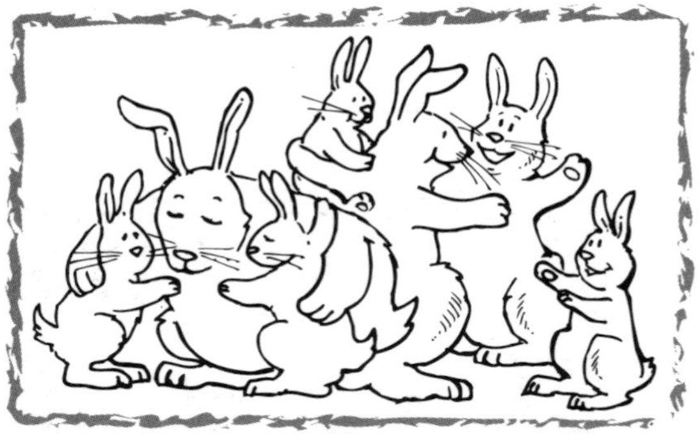

relatives

reunion

You see relatives at a reunion.

23 Daily Handwriting Practice Thursday

The Family Reunion

Happy smiles,
Lots of names,
Yummy food,
Crazy games,
Hugs and kisses,
Teary eyes,
Handshakes, backslaps,
Warm good-byes.

Copy the poem.

71

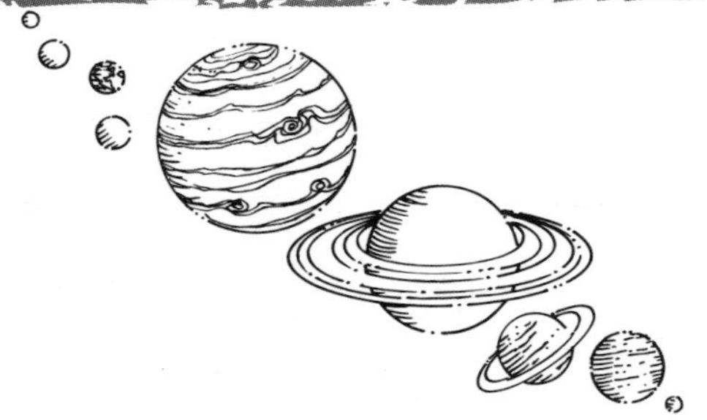

Name:

our solar system

nine planets and one sun

24 Daily Handwriting Practice Monday

These planets are smaller than Earth.

Name:

Pluto

Mars

Mercury

Venus

24 Daily Handwriting Practice Tuesday

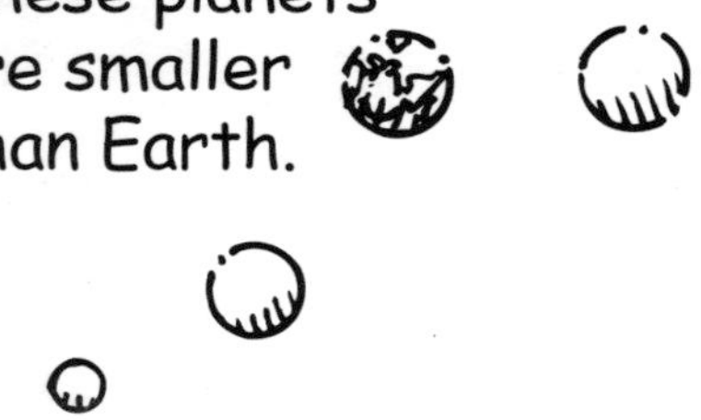

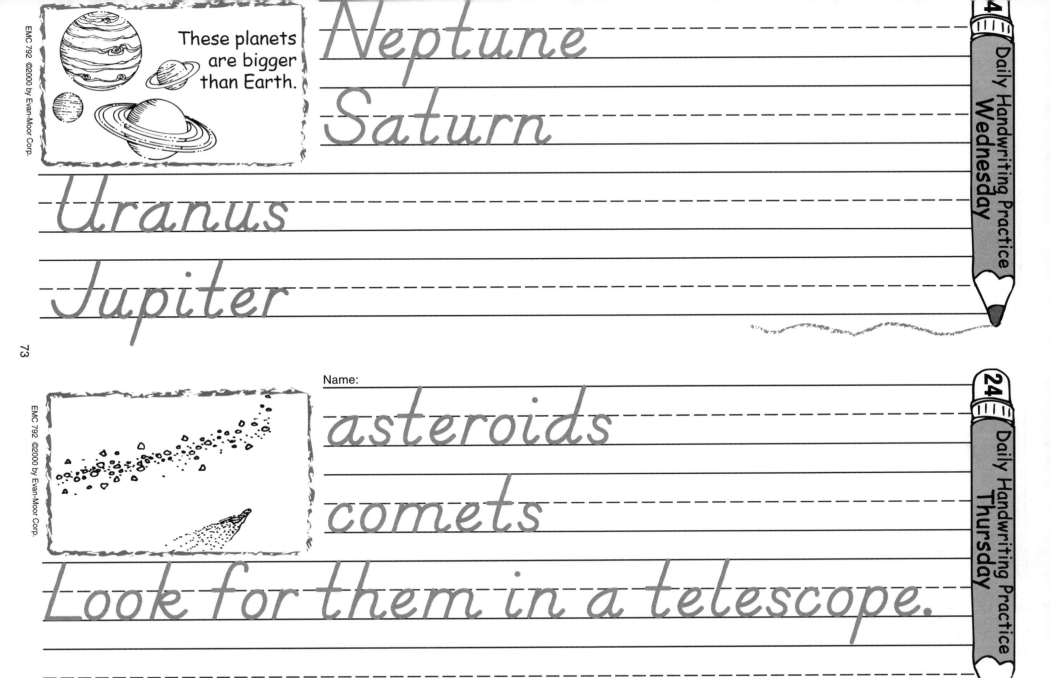

These planets are bigger than Earth.

Neptune

Saturn

Uranus

Jupiter

Name:

asteroids

comets

Look for them in a telescope.

Name: _____

Write the names of the planets.

Our Solar System

1. Mercury

2. Venus

3. Earth

4. Mars

5. Jupiter

6. Saturn

7. Uranus

8. Neptune

9. Pluto

74

1 _____ a small, rocky planet

2 _____ covered in thick, yellow clouds

3 _____ third planet from the sun

4 _____ soil is full of rust-colored iron dust

5 _____ largest planet in the solar system

6 _____ rings made of ice and rock

7 _____ 5 large moons and 10 small moons

8 _____ ball of gas with a center of rock

9 _____ smaller than the Earth's moon

There are
12 months
every year.
See how well I write
them here.

The first three
months are:

January

February

March

75

Name:

There are
12 months
every year.
See how well I write
them here.

The next three
months are:

April

May

June

There are
12 months
every year.
See how well I write
them here.

The next three
months are:

July

August

September

There are
12 months
every year.
See how well I write
them here.

The last three
months are:

October

November

December

Name: _____

The Calendar

Write the names of the months in order.

May   January   August
December   July   November
June   October   February
April   September   March

77

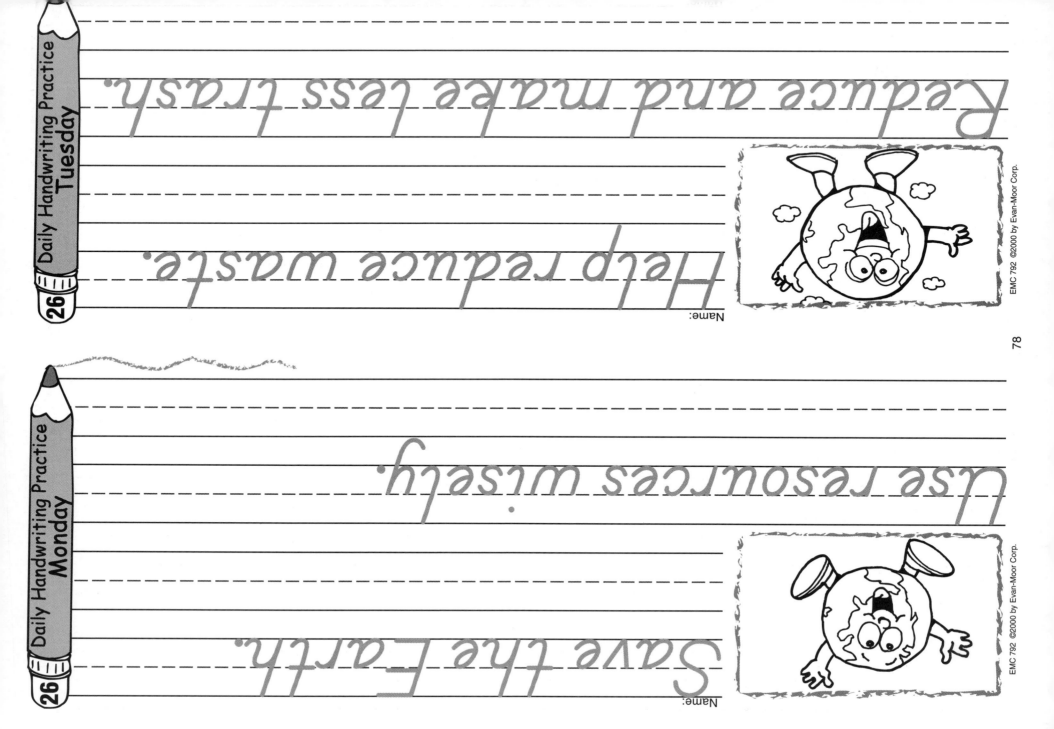

Reduce and make less trash.

Help reduce waste.

Name:

EMC 792 ©2000 by Evan-Moor Corp.

Use resources wisely.

Save the Earth.

Name:

EMC 792 ©2000 by Evan-Moor Corp.

Name:

Reuse old things.

Turn trash into treasures.

79

Name:

Recycle your trash.

Make the old into new.

Name: _____

Save
the Earth

Make a plan for helping to protect our environment.
Write what you will do. Use your best handwriting.

80

I will reduce.

I will reuse.

I will recycle.

I will _____ .

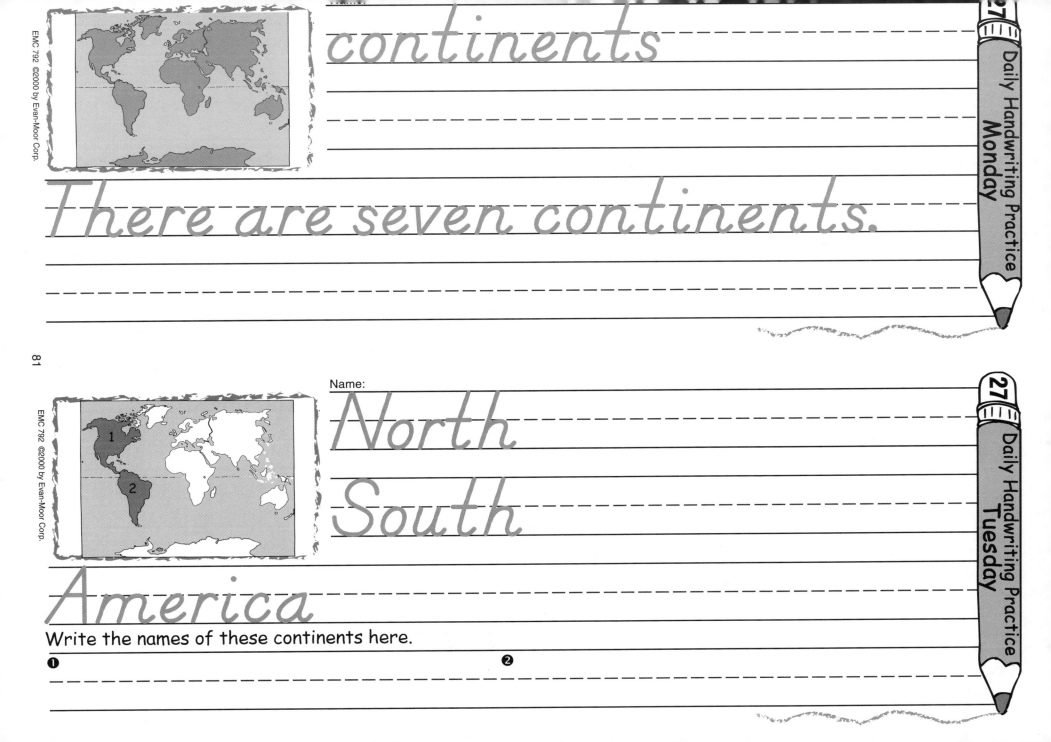

continents

There are seven continents.

81

Name:

North

South

America

Write the names of these continents here.

❶

❷

EMC 792 ©2000 by Evan-Moor Corp.

Name:

Australia

Antarctica

Write the names of these continents here.

❸   ❹

EMC 792 ©2000 by Evan-Moor Corp.

Name:

Asia

Europe

Africa

Write the names of these continents here.

❺   ❻   ❼

Name: _____

Label the continents.

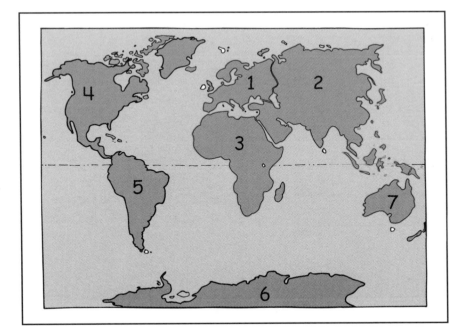

Africa   Antarctica
North America   Asia
South America   Australia
Europe

83

1 _____

2 _____

3 _____

4 _____

5 _____

6 _____

7 _____

On which continent do you live?
_____

I live on   .

EMC 792 ©2000 by Evan-Moor Corp.

Name:

The outside layer of the Earth is called the crust.

crust

rock

soil

Rock and soil form the crust.

84

EMC 792 ©2000 by Evan-Moor Corp.

Name:

The mantle is made of rock and metal.

mantle

mantle

metal

The mantle is below the crust.

EMC 792 ©2000 by Evan-Moor Corp.

The core is under the mantle.

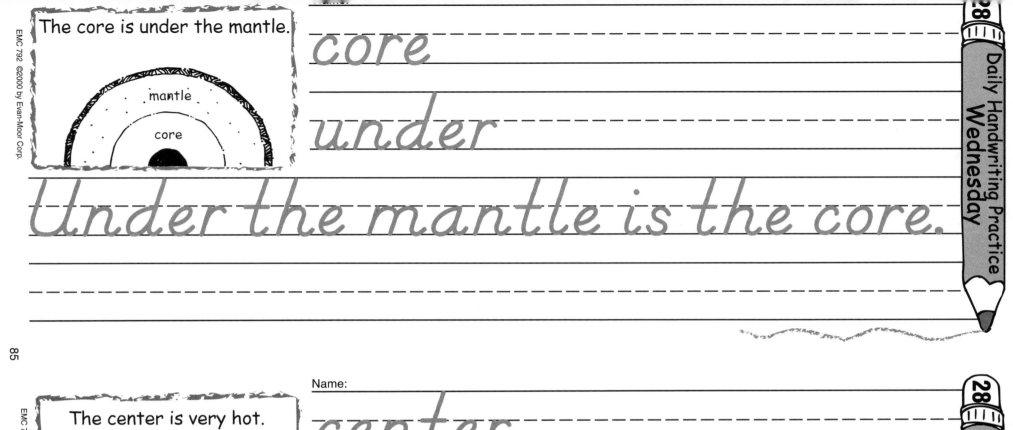

core

under

Under the mantle is the core.

85

EMC 792 ©2000 by Evan-Moor Corp.

The center is very hot.

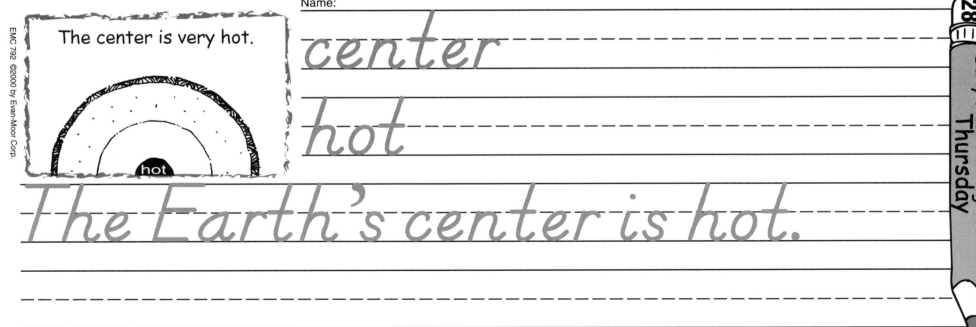

Name:

center

hot

The Earth's center is hot.

Name: _____

Label the Earth's layers.

1 _____

1 -

_____

2 -

_____

3 -

_____

4 -

_____

86

We walk on the Earth's _____

. _____

- -

_____

crust   _core_   _mantle_   _center_

Day or night,
We need light.

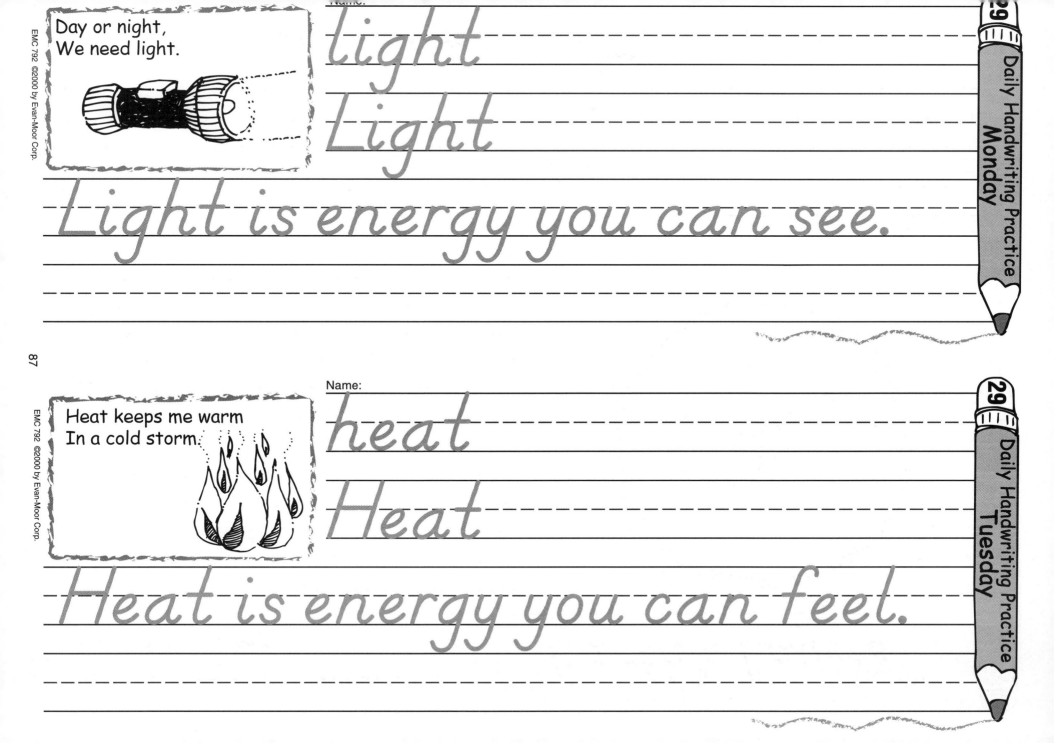

light

Light

Light is energy you can see.

EMC 792 ©2000 by Evan-Moor Corp.

Name:

29

Daily Handwriting Practice
Tuesday

Heat keeps me warm
In a cold storm.

heat

Heat

Heat is energy you can feel.

EMC 792 ©2000 by Evan-Moor Corp.

Name:

Just use your ear.
It's loud and clear.

sound

Sound

Sound is energy you can hear.

EMC 792 ©2000 by Evan-Moor Corp.

Name:

Light, heat, and sound are all forms of energy.

energy

Energy

Energy has different forms.

EMC 792 ©2000 by Evan-Moor Corp.

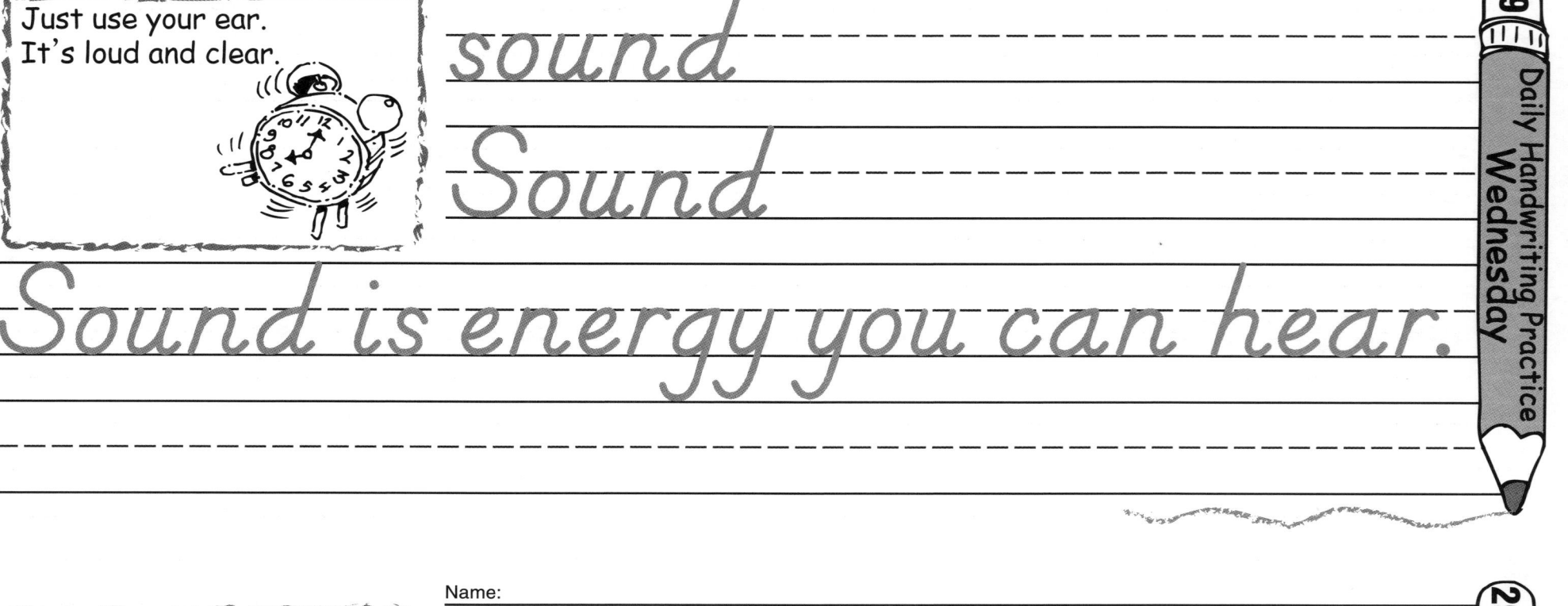

Energy Is All Around Us

Energy is all around us.
The light you see is energy.
The sound you hear is energy.
The heat you feel is energy.
Energy is all around us.

Copy the information.

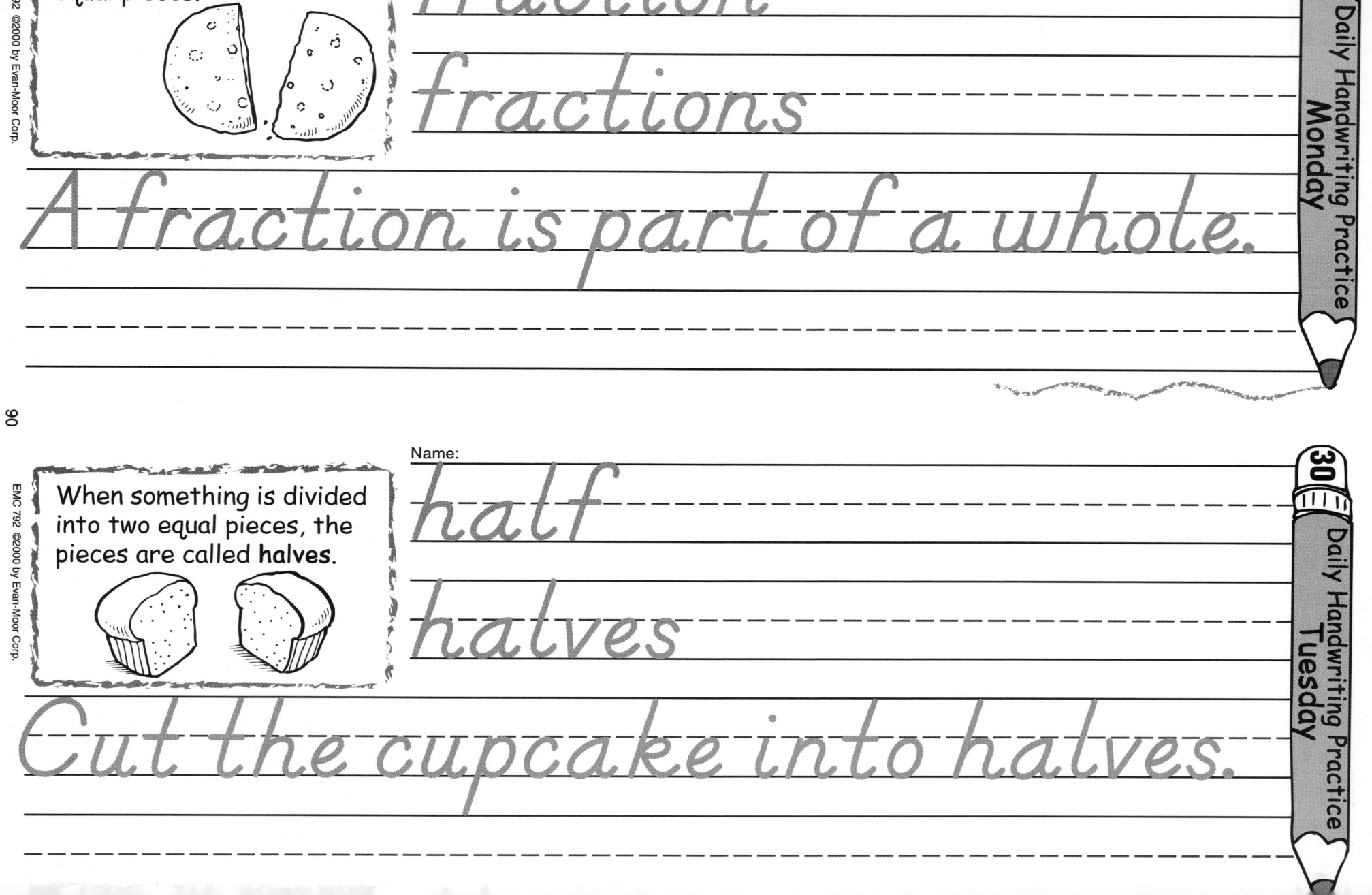

Fractions have to be equal pieces.

Name:

fraction

fractions

A fraction is part of a whole.

EMC 792 ©2000 by Evan-Moor Corp.

90

When something is divided into two equal pieces, the pieces are called **halves**.

Name:

half

halves

Cut the cupcake into halves.

EMC 792 ©2000 by Evan-Moor Corp.

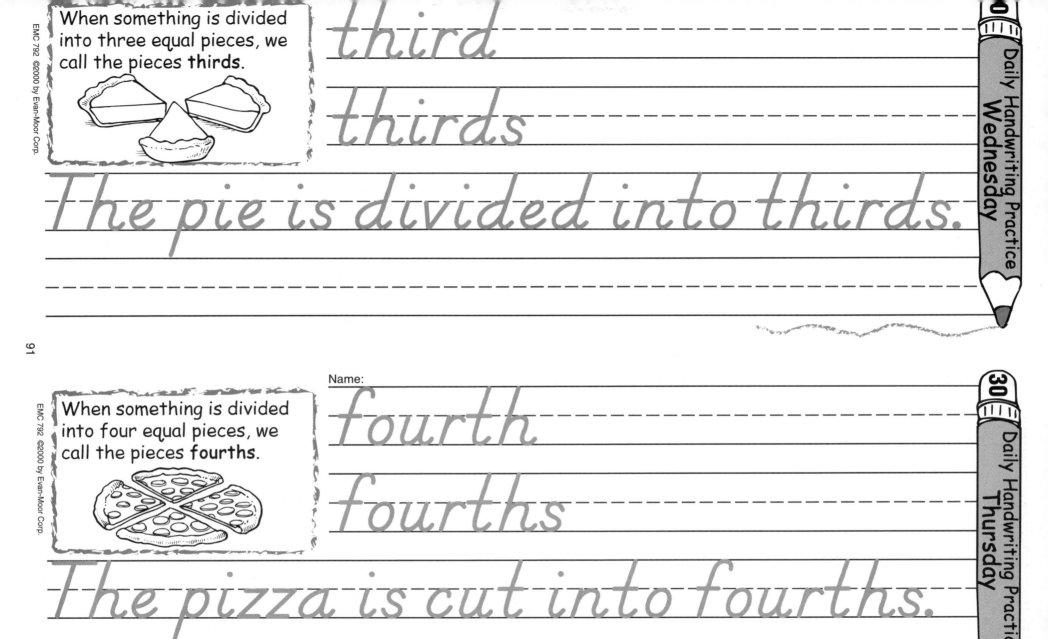

EMC 792 ©2000 by Evan-Moor Corp.

When something is divided into three equal pieces, we call the pieces **thirds**.

third

thirds

The pie is divided into thirds.

91

Name:

EMC 792 ©2000 by Evan-Moor Corp.

When something is divided into four equal pieces, we call the pieces **fourths**.

fourth

fourths

The pizza is cut into fourths.

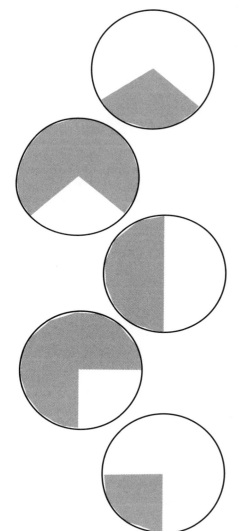

Name: _____

Fractions

one-half   one-fourth   one-third   two-thirds   three-fourths

Write how much is shaded.

Daily Handwriting Practice
Friday
30

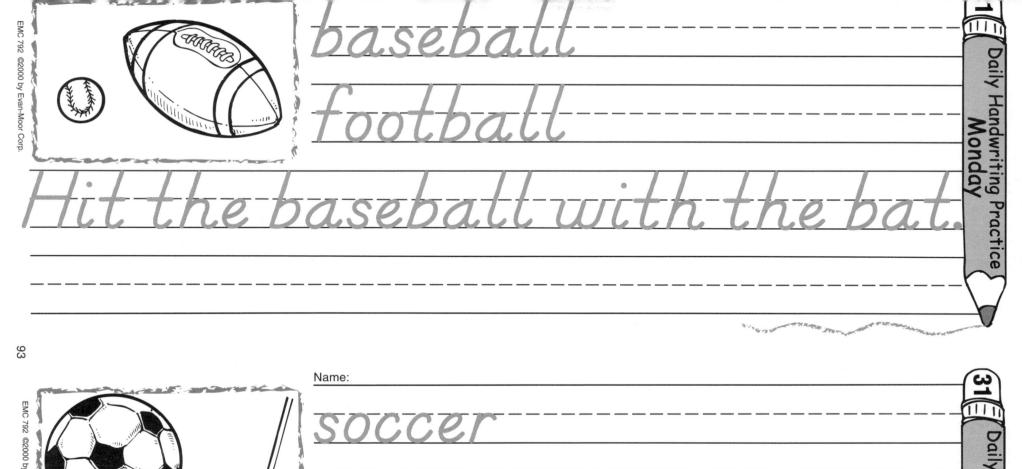

baseball

football

Hit the baseball with the bat.

93

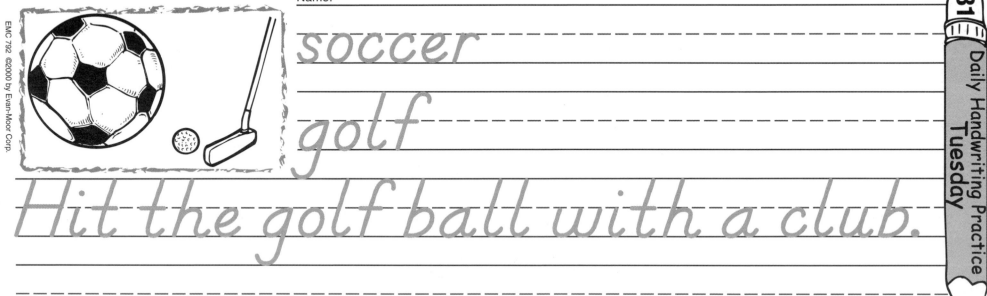

Name:

soccer

golf

Hit the golf ball with a club.

31 Daily Handwriting Practice Wednesday

Name:

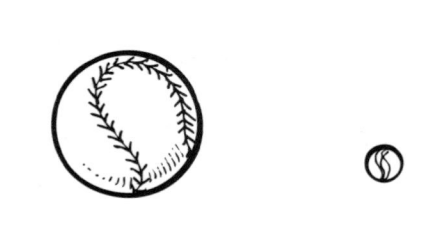

softball

marble

One ball is big. One is little.

31 Daily Handwriting Practice Thursday

Name:

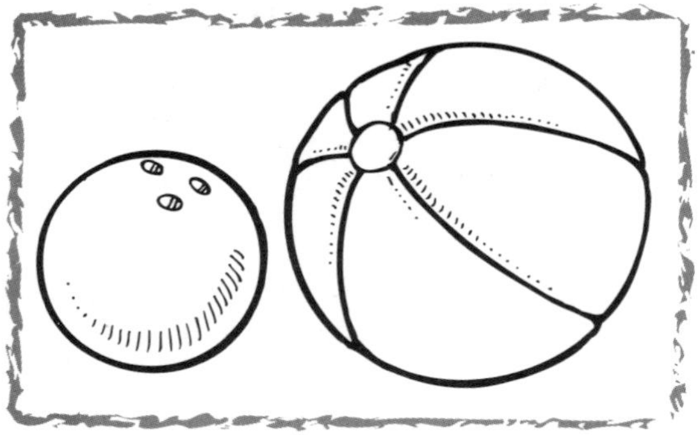

bowling

beach

One ball is soft. One is hard.

Copy the poem.

Let's Play Ball!

95

Hit them. Catch them.
Throw them back.
Hike them to the
Quarterback.

Kick them. Roll them.
Blow them up.
Putt them into the
Little cup.

Name:

Roll out the clay.
It's time to play.

roll

flatten

I can flatten my clay.

96

Name:

Make a long snake
Or a pat-a-cake.

coil

fold

I can shape my clay pot.

Bake your project
in the sun
Or in an oven when
you're done.

bake

fire

I can bake my clay.

EMC 792 ©2000 by Evan-Moor Corp.

Name:

Brush on the shine.
It looks mighty fine.

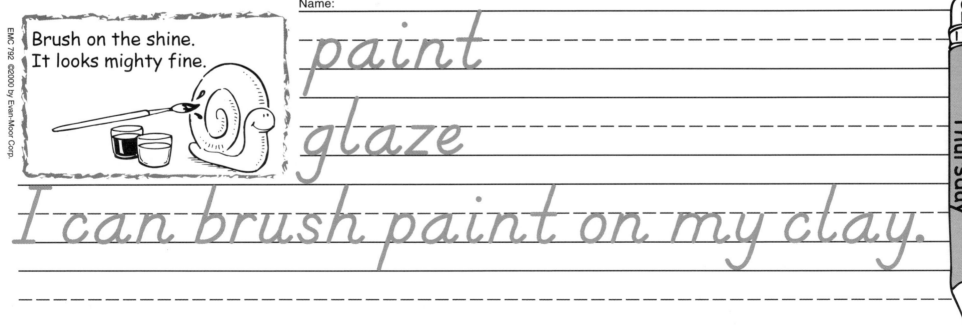

paint

glaze

I can brush paint on my clay.

EMC 792 ©2000 by Evan-Moor Corp.

Name: _____

Baker's Clay

What You Need

- *bowl*
- *spoon*
- *4 scoops of flour*
- *1 scoop of salt*
- *1 ½ scoops of warm water*

What You Do

1. Dissolve the salt in warm water.
2. Stir as you add the flour.
3. Knead the dough for 5 minutes.
4. Put the dough into a plastic bag.

Copy the steps here that tell what to do.

1. _____

2. _____

3. _____

4. _____

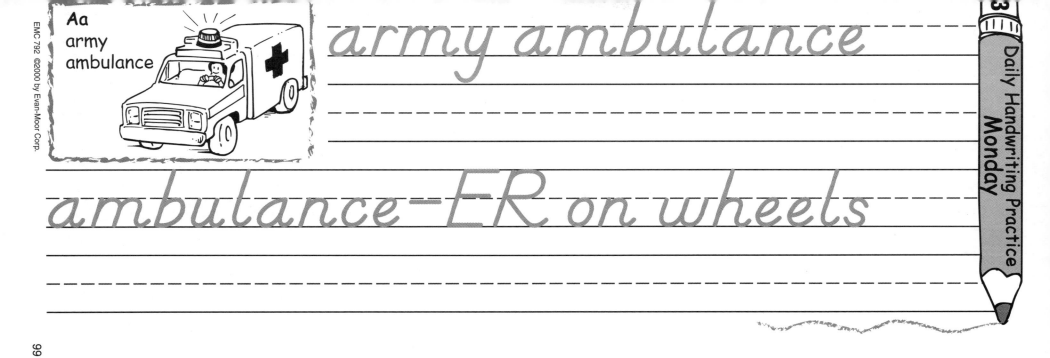

Aa
army
ambulance

army ambulance

ambulance-ER on wheels

99

Bb
big
bulldozer

Name:

big bulldozer

The bulldozer breaks up brush.

Cc
cozy
carriage

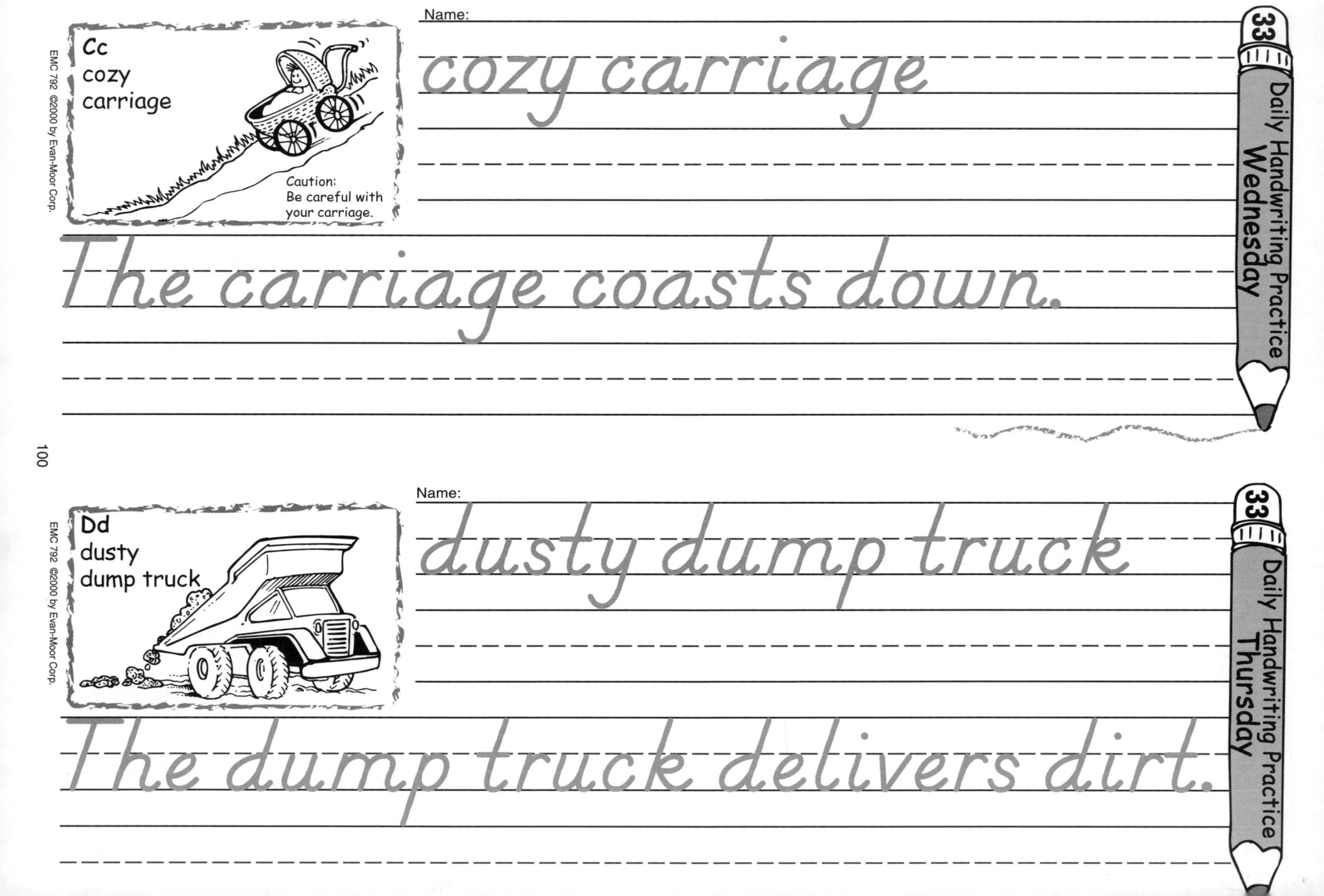

Caution:
Be careful with
your carriage.

Name:

cozy carriage

The carriage coasts down.

100

Dd
dusty
dump truck

Name:

dusty dump truck

The dump truck delivers dirt.

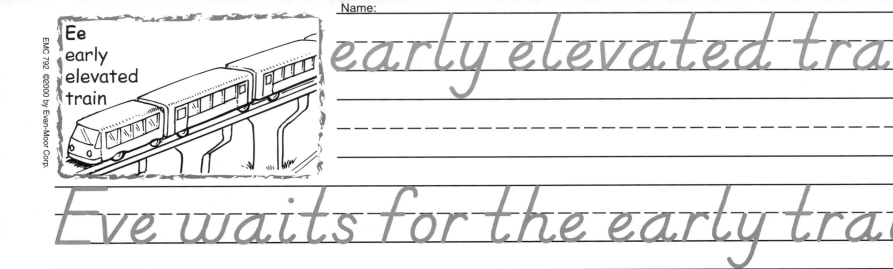

Name:

Ee
early
elevated
train

early elevated train

Eve waits for the early train.

EMC 792 ©2000 by Evan-Moor Corp.

Ff
fancy
forklift

Name:

fancy forklift

Follow the forklift forward.

EMC 792 ©2000 by Evan-Moor Corp.

EMC 792 ©2000 by Evan-Moor Corp.

Gg
gas-gulping
go-cart

Name:

gas-gulping go-cart

Get some gas for the go-cart.

EMC 792 ©2000 by Evan-Moor Corp.

Hh
high-flying
helicopter

Name:

helicopter

The helicopter hovers nearby.

Ii
important
icebreaker

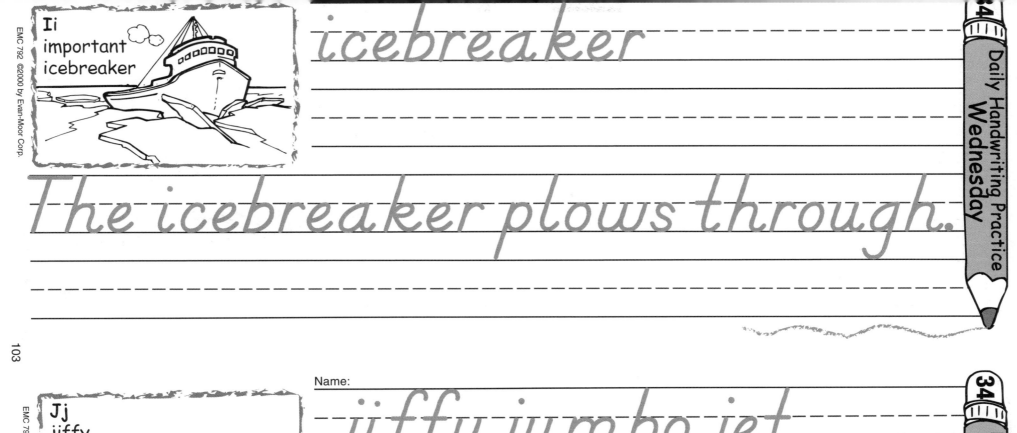

icebreaker

The icebreaker plows through.

103

Jj
jiffy
jumbo
jet

Name:

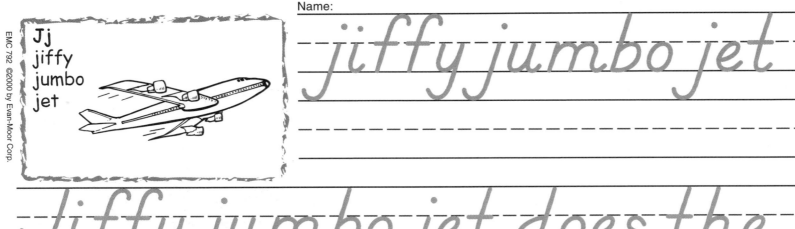

jiffy jumbo jet

Jiffy jumbo jet does the job.

The limousine led the line.

long limousine

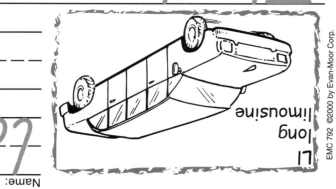

Ll long limousine

Name:

A kayak is a kind of canoe.

keen kayak

Kk keen kayak

Name:

Mm
Mom's
motorcycle

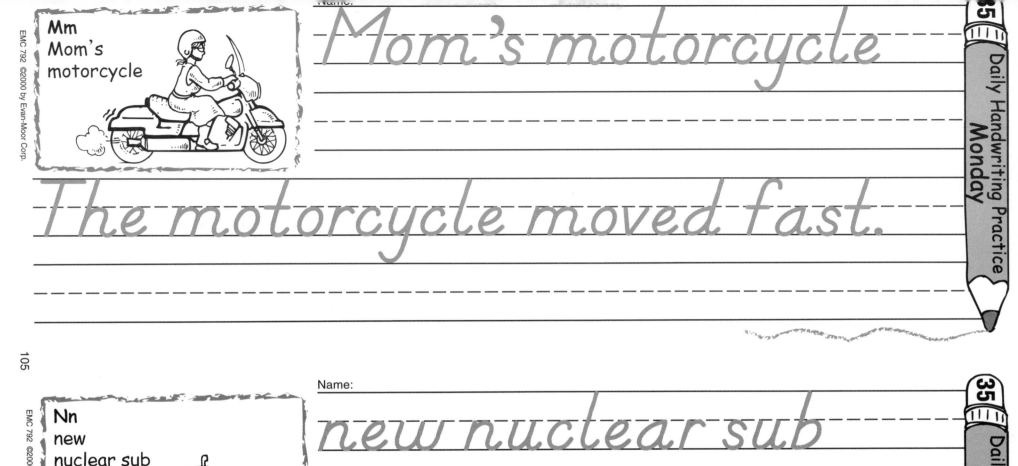

Name:

Mom's motorcycle

The motorcycle moved fast.

Nn
new
nuclear sub

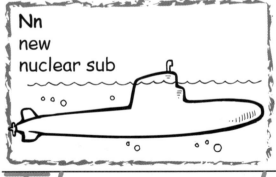

Name:

new nuclear sub

The nuclear sub navigated.

EMC 792 ©2000 by Evan-Moor Corp.

Oo
orange
oil tanker

Name:

orange oil tanker

The oil tanker sailed to sea.

106

EMC 792 ©2000 by Evan-Moor Corp.

Pp
purple
pickup

Name:

purple pickup

The pup rode in the pickup.

Name:

Qq
auiet
QE II

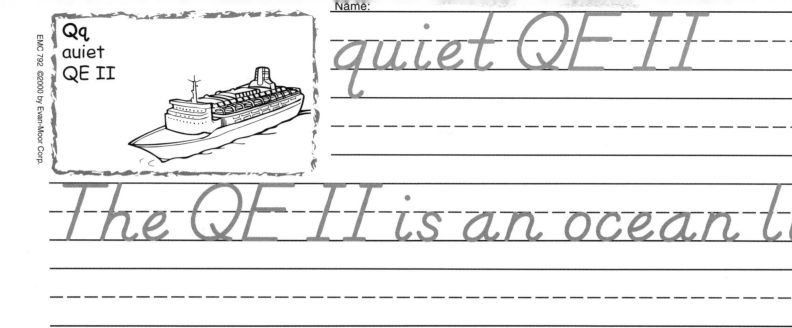

quiet QE II

The QE II is an ocean liner.

Name:

Rr
racing
roadster

racing roadster

The roadster raced up a road.

36

Daily Handwriting Practice
Monday

Ss
strong
steamroller

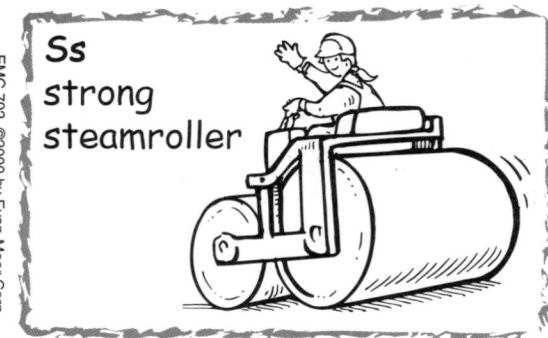

Name:

strong steamroller

Steamroller squashes the soil.

36

Daily Handwriting Practice
Tuesday

Tt
tall
trolley

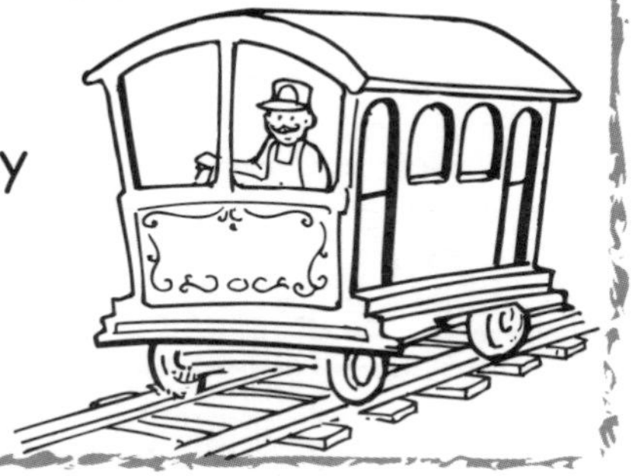

Name:

tall trolley

Trolley travels on the tracks.

Uu
useful
unicycle

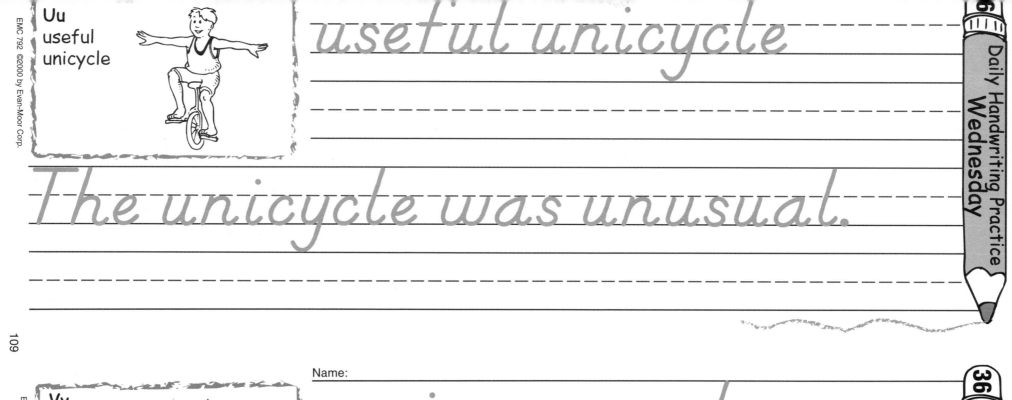

useful unicycle

The unicycle was unusual.

Daily Handwriting Practice
Wednesday

109

Vv
various
vessels

Name:

various vessels

Vessels transport passengers.

Daily Handwriting Practice
Thursday

The XK120 is a sports car.

exciting XK120

Xx

exciting
XK120

Name:

Wheelbarrow helps me work.

white wheelbarrow

Ww

white
wheelbarrow

Name:

EMC 792 ©2000 by Evan-Moor Corp.

Yy
yellow
yacht

yellow yacht

Yvette yearns for the yacht.

Name:

EMC 792 ©2000 by Evan-Moor Corp.

Zz
zooming
Zero

zooming Zero

The Zero is a real plane.

My Vehicle Alphabet Book

This ABC Book of Vehicles represents my
best handwriting. I have practiced writing
(and reading) all of the alphabet in lots of
different words.

My name is _____.

I dedicate this book to _____.

— fold —